I'm Not Like Everybody Else

T0350070

SERIES EDITORS · *Marco Abel and Roland Végső*

PROV
OCAT
IONS

Something in the world forces us to think.
—Gilles Deleuze

The world provokes thought. Thinking is nothing but the human response to this provocation. Thus, the very nature of thought is to be the product of a provocation. This is why a genuine act of provocation cannot be the empty rhetorical gesture of the contrarian. It must be an experimental response to the historical necessity to act. Unlike the contrarian, we refuse to reduce provocation to a passive noun or a state of being. We believe that real moments of provocation are constituted by a series of actions that are best defined by verbs or even infinitives—verbs in a modality of potentiality, of the promise of action. To provoke is to intervene in the present by invoking an as yet undecided future radically different from what is declared to be possible in the present and, in so doing, to arouse the desire for bringing about change. By publishing short books from multiple disciplinary perspectives that are closer to the genres of the manifesto, the polemical essay, the intervention, and the pamphlet than to traditional scholarly monographs, "Provocations" hopes to serve as a forum for the kind of theoretical experimentation that we consider to be the very essence of thought.

www.provocationsbooks.com

I'm Not Like Everybody Else

Biopolitics, Neoliberalism, and American Popular Music

JEFFREY T. NEALON

UNIVERSITY OF NEBRASKA PRESS · LINCOLN AND LONDON

The series editors would like to thank James
Brunton, Daniel Clausen, Robert Lipscomb,
Dillon Rockrohr, Jessica Tebo, and Colten
White for their work on the manuscript.

Library of Congress Cataloging-
in-Publication Data
Names: Nealon, Jeffrey T.
(Jeffrey Thomas) author.
Title: I'm not like everybody else:
biopolitics, neoliberalism, and American
popular music / Jeffrey T. Nealon.
Description: Lincoln: University of Nebraska
Press, [2018]. | Series: Provocations
Identifiers: LCCN 2017056179
ISBN 9781496208651 (pbk.: alk. paper)
ISBN 9781496210951 (epub)
ISBN 9781496210968 (mobi)
ISBN 9781496210975 (pdf)
Subjects: LCSH: Popular music—Political
aspects—United States. | Neoliberalism—
United States. | Biopolitics—United States.
Classification: LCC ML3917.U6 N43 2018 |
DDC 781.640973—dc23 LC record available
at https://lccn.loc.gov/2017056179

Set in Sorts Mill Goudy by Mikala R Kolander.
Designed by N. Putens.

CONTENTS

ACKNOWLEDGMENTS

More than anything else I've written, this book owes a large number of debts spread out over a long time span. To the press questionnaire's query, "What special qualifications do you have to write this book?" I have to admit I simply answered, "I've been intently listening to American popular music my entire life."

Some of my earliest memories are of listening to eight-track tapes in my parents' car (*Eddy Arnold's Greatest Hits* and a lot of Glen Campbell). My sister would routinely buy me 45s (Helen Reddy's "I Am Woman" was probably the most memorable), while my soon-to-be brother-in-law assured me that the group Aliotta Haynes Jeremiah was the future of American music. Those family members are all gone now, but they live on in and around the music.

My musical tastes began to take shape in high school. I still see my group of friends from that time and keep listening to new music with them (though a lot of oldies do get played at that yearly get-together). I especially recall seeing an epic Jeff Beck show with Rich Babjak, James Brown at Summerfest in Milwaukee with Mike Maicke, the Allman Brothers with George Carens, Talking Heads with Greg Roman, and Sippie Wallace with Thane Bauz. Those long discussions and listening hours in various friends' basements laid the groundwork for this book.

In college and grad school I most intensely remember seeing the Pogues on Saint Patrick's Day with Ann Gunkel, Cat Power with Joe Sullivan, and Fred Frith with Murray Coffey, between stops at the Green Mill with Sherry Brennan to see Von Freeman. I very keenly remember seeing Eric (Blowtorch) Beaumont play several times. I'm pretty sure I went to some Grateful Dead shows with Tim White, Margaret Sullivan, Jennifer Fettig, and Mark Nadeau, but I can't be positive. While I never made it to a Dead show with Michael Naas, we did get to see Godspeed You! Black Emperor, and that's pretty close.

I owe a major debt of gratitude to the Penn State students who took the graduate and undergraduate courses that I offered in the lead-up to this writing. I'd also like to thank my theory colleagues Frida Beckman, Kevin DeLuca, Rich Doyle, Grant Farred, Gregg Flaxman, Aaron Jaffe, Gregg Lambert, Ulf Olsson, and Cary Wolfe, to whom I've prattled on about these topics for the past few years. Likewise, a special thank you to the editors of the Provocations series, Marco Abel (with whom I have a friendly ongoing musical taste war) and Roland Végső (who played me some delightfully unlistenable Hungarian music at his house very late one night).

Finally, Leisha and I took in our first show together in Chicago, Marc Ribot y Los Cubanos Postizos. Several years later we took an in-utero Bram to his first show, the Flaming Lips, on New Year's Eve 2000, and Dash and I have been to several memorable experimental music nights here in State College. My family continues to suffer my complete monopolizing of music in the household, so while this book is a sort of concept album that's meant for everyone, in the end it's dedicated to Leisha, Bram, and Dash.

The Music (Discourse) Must Change!

The ways that we think about popular music haven't changed substantially since Adorno and Benjamin set the terms for these popular-culture debates in the 1930s: either popular music is a standardized, sold-out commodity leading to mass conformity, or popular music (or more accurately, some benighted music that rises above the commodified fray) can offer a kind of authentic individual identity or resistant group reaction against those very dictates of consumption capitalism. Trying to think beyond that cultural studies dead end, this book holds the following truths to be (nearly) self-evident:

Resist Musical Authenticity Discourse!

A norm-busting musical authenticity discourse no longer functions against the grain of our neoliberal, biopolitical world. Ironically, that's the case *not* because music has finally and completely been co-opted by the capitalist Man. Rather biopolitical capitalism has in recent decades found an organizing use for values of musical authenticity, a neoliberal world where my musical tastes help demonstrate that "I'm Not Like Everybody Else."

Attend to the Uses and Abuses of Music!

As the songs and artists are neither commodified nor authentic, it's the *uses* of popular music to which we must now attend—uses completely revolutionized by the ubiquity of smartphone playlists and internet streams.

Mood, not Meaning!

Popular music no longer offers individuals *meaning*, but functions as a kind of mood-altering machine, an alternative series of flows on the sea of 24/7 attention capitalism.

Sound, Not Vision!

We all wonder sometimes, but this book argues that sound is more important than vision as a bellwether for thinking about cultural production today.

I'm Not Like Everybody Else

Introduction

This book has a dual origin—first in a provocation, and then in a subsequent thought experiment. The provocation comes in a single line from Lawrence Grossberg, the dean of cultural studies scholars of popular music. Looking back on the field in his 2002 essay, "Reflections of a Disappointed Popular Music Scholar," Grossberg wrote that especially where it pertains to critical theory, "I do not think that writing about popular music has significantly changed (to say nothing of 'progressed') in forty years."[1] Well, I think to myself, let's see if, more than a decade later, we can do something about that (and the recent emergence of "sound studies" has gone a long way toward offering consistency to the field). Second, the thought experiment: what if we take popular music to be the *spine* of American cultural production in the late twentieth century (and beyond), rather than treating it as the frivolous younger sibling of literature, museum art, classical music, art-house cinema, or architecture? If we take popular music seriously as artistic production, if we follow popular music on its own terms rather than comparing it (unfavorably) to other art forms, what happens to the cultural stories we've told ourselves about the latter part of the American twentieth century—about art versus commodity, high versus mass culture, artistic authenticity versus sold-out popularity?

In short, *I'm Not Like Everybody Else* attempts to rethink recent American cultural production through a primary, unapologetic emphasis on the history of popular music.

Of course, many critics over recent decades have suggested that popular music should be taken seriously (or at least as seriously as other art forms), though the current reigning paradigm for music criticism, so-called "poptimism," suggests that evaluating music's artistic success involves wide-ranging appreciation more than it does critical analysis. Against that trend, I want to begin not simply by throwing open the gates ("It's all good," poptimism's slogan), but by looking yet again at the early twentieth-century work of Theodor Adorno, to revisit the reasons why scholars *didn't* take popular music seriously for many, many years: because of the structuring opposition that runs through much of the cultural criticism of the twentieth century—high culture versus mass culture.[2] Or more simply, twentieth-century thinking about cultural production was divided between "authentic" art and the "inauthentic" commodity, and Adorno solidifies this line of inquiry. If you look at popular music through Adorno's eyes, almost all you'll find is degraded schlock put out by an industry that's eager to please or merely distract its consumers (Adorno sometimes calls them "victims"), rather than a music that will challenge the listener or further help to innovate musical forms. For Adorno, popular music certainly has effects, but those effects are uniformly negative, feeding a herd mentality of mass-produced sameness rather than heading in the opposite direction, toward autonomous, resistant individuality. As Adorno argues in "On Popular Music," these tunes are "composed in such a way that the process of translation of the unique into the norm is already planned and, to a certain extent, achieved within the composition itself. The composition hears for the listener. This is how popular music divests the listener of his spontaneity and promotes conditioned reflexes."[3]

I begin by revisiting Adorno's dismissive critique because I'm keen to point out that when recent sympathetic critics do begin taking popular music seriously, they all of course argue against Adorno; but many critics of popular music also continue to follow Adorno in an odd, subterranean way. The nearly ubiquitous move in work that takes pop music seriously is to suggest that there's something of "high culture" that's been missed in the "mass culture" forms of popular music—that Elvis Presley or Johnny Rotten are in some way also great artists and thinkers, just like Marcel Duchamp (Edward Comentale's comparison for Elvis in his fine book *Sweet Air*) or Guy Debord and the Situationists (Greil Marcus's comparison for the Sex Pistols in *Lipstick Traces*). Which is to say, the move in popular music criticism is often to take the objects or artists as "seriously" as other high-culture artifacts, to reveal a hidden artistic genius in their work, or to show how popular music does indeed, contra Adorno, offer a norm-challenging brand of subjectivity—a certain kind of resistant push against the herd mentality of mass culture.

This all seems perfectly legitimate to me, but is likewise the ironic point where music critics tacitly agree with Adorno's premise concerning popular culture: that seriousness, or greatness, or some kind of authenticity-based negating function (saying "no" to mainstream values) is the key to artistic worthiness. The most spectacular version of this tendency in popular music criticism is probably Christopher Ricks's book dedicated to close-reading Bob Dylan lyrics (*Dylan's Visions of Sin*), which positions the singer as nothing less than a contemporary American Milton. Yale University Press's 900-page *Rap Anthology*, however, makes a strong case that, while not exactly Milton, rap and hip-hop are the bellwether lyrical genres of our time.

Also in this "elevate the popular" mode, there are the ubiquitous (at least at my local Barnes & Noble) books published by Open Court in their Popular Culture and Philosophy series: *The Beatles and Philosophy*, *Led Zeppelin and Philosophy*, *Johnny Cash and Philosophy*, and so on. Likewise, Continuum's 33⅓ series of books puts on display for us the hidden importance of Liz Phair's *Exile in Guyville* for understanding third-wave feminism, or offers us thoughts on the importance of Sly and the Family Stone for thinking about the birth of multiculturalism in the 1970s.[4]

While I'm happy to talk about or even "interpret" individual songs, albums, and artists according to larger philosophical, historical, and social trends (and I'll certainly do some of that), the argumentative maneuver that will interest me in *I'm Not Like Everybody Else* is the opposite of this elevation move: I'm not going to scour Snoop Dogg's records looking for enjambment or undecidability or affect or references to contemporary racial tensions or his depiction of animals or some other critical or philosophical theme. In other words, I'm not interested in making songs and artists into interpretive puzzles or society-challenging statements, rendering them "worthy" of high-culture explication.

Rather, it's the everyday "mass culture" quality of popular music that will interest me; in addition, it's this ubiquity that to my mind makes popular music the skeleton key to understanding American cultural production over the second half of the twentieth century. In a nutshell, my approach will suggest that popular music is important and influential precisely because of its daily level of cultural saturation over the past decades. I will argue that popular music is in fact the twentieth century's most significant art form if we're looking for an accurate barometer of cultural subject- or identity-production in America. In terms of its cultural impact and scope, popular music has been significant for the cultural life of the United States, much more so than museum art or literature, because pop music is so enmeshed within the functioning of everyday life.

This book takes off from several recent works in sound studies and technology studies (most specifically, Anahid Kassabian's *Ubiquitous Listening* and Jonathan Sterne's *MP3: The Meaning of a Format*) that have begun to move the field away from looking at individual works as the privileged unit of music criticism (whether the song, the album, the live concert, the genre, or the career of an individual artist) to think instead about listening practices themselves and how they've been refashioned over recent decades by changes in technology and society. In *MP3* Sterne calls attention to the fact that we tend to see the history of American popular music as a series of innovative musical trends, groups, or styles: for example, from the first wave of rock, miraculously born in 1955; through the folk revival of the early sixties; to the second wave of rock in the mid- to late sixties; all the way through soul, punk, disco, and new wave in the seventies and eighties; hip-hop and rap in the nineties; grunge, emo, and so on. Which is to say we see or remember pop music history as being driven by *people* (particular performers or bands) and their innovative, authentic "genius." But as Sterne reminds us, the history of popular music is also a history of technological and economic changes in the twentieth century, a history of sound and formatting technologies (the transistor radio or the portable record player, the 78, 45, and 33 rpm record, the jukebox, the cassette, the Walkman, the CD, the MP3, the computer, file-sharing software, the iPod, the smartphone, streaming music services, YouTube, etc.). And as Sterne's subtitle, *The Meaning of a Format*, makes clear, the technological history of recording, compressing, and selling music makes a great deal of difference in the history of what that music *is*, how people consume and use it, and ultimately on what music *means* to the people who listen to it.

Although they might contain many of the same songs and artists, an album collection of the 1970s and an MP3 library of the twenty-first century have substantially different vectors of cultural "meaning." They are curated differently by collectors; they're accessible quite differently (even if you had a portable record player, you couldn't play an LP album on the bus); and they produce artistic and lifestyle effects in very different ways. For example, as someone who had quite a number of albums in the 1970s, I would point out that you can't deseed your stash with a CD or an MP3; but an album with a foldout cover—I'd suggest Jimi Hendrix's live album *Band of Gypsys*—will do the trick quite nicely. Though I understand weed doesn't so much have seeds anymore, so maybe it's a moot point.

In any case, as we'll see throughout, technology matters decisively in this story of artistic invention: from the jazz and swing of the twenties and thirties (distributed on 78s and played live on the radio) to the Rock1 of the midfifties (where the 45 rpm single was the key distribution vehicle); through folk to the Rock2 or "classic rock" of the album-oriented sixties and seventies; to the punk, disco, and new wave of the eighties (most of it distributed on cassettes); the grunge, hip-hop, and rap distributed largely on CDs in the nineties; right up through the explosion of genres and forms over the past ten years (myriad niche musical forms—everything from death metal to K-pop) that circulate largely through electronic means like MP3 file sharing, YouTube, and streaming services. Even while Grossberg insists that the discourse surrounding popular music hasn't changed much (it's long been about "keeping it real" in one way or another), the technologies by which such artistic authenticity is rendered and consumed have changed quickly and decisively over the last few decades. The MP3, for example, has made the Rock2 practice of listening to a complete album (on the analogy of reading a book) nearly obsolete. In practice, the MP3 has nearly made paying to own recorded music a thing of the past as well, and thereby we see concretely the ways a change in the dominant recording and distribution format for popular music can take down nearly an entire industry in one technological swoop. In short, with changes in musical technology and portability, there emerge parallel changes in how popular music—and popular music discourse about artistic authenticity—functions in the twenty-first century.

In fact, the most central argument of this book is that "authenticity" as a musical category—and indeed as a larger category for understanding the workings of subjectivity—did at some point crucially function "against the grain" in the midtwentieth century (in the folk and Rock2 eras); but maybe the most obvious problem surrounding music consumption today is that authenticity—that great twentieth-century bulwark against "selling out"—is probably *the* fetish commodity of twenty-first-century neoliberal capitalism. Just Google the words "authenticity" and "business" and you'll get the complete tutorial: marketing in the twenty-first century depends on the patina of authenticity—some heady mix of a brand's originality, innovation, and a deep personal connection to the product (against the vulgar bottom line of profits and mass-produced sameness). It's this seeming commitment to individual authenticity that has underwritten the major business success stories of the past few decades: everything from electronics giant Apple to sharing sites like Facebook, all the way to microbreweries and pop-up stores. And this fetish for authenticity conversely explains why venerable American stores like Sears or Kmart (brands with zero street cred) have quietly disappeared from the local mall.

It's here in authenticity-land that we begin to see how the neoliberal consumption logic of the twenty-first century oddly finds its roots in the countercultural popular musics of the twentieth century and pop music fans' almost slavish dedication to the authenticity of their music, whatever genre or style it may be (new country has hard-core fans, just as gangsta rap does). In short, I'll be arguing that this cultural authenticity discourse—and its signature "way cool/sold out" dialectic—has migrated from its home turf of popular music discourse and practice to become something like the logic of the whole in the American present. This strongly held yet constantly updating sense of musical taste and identity (born in fan discourse of the twentieth century) has morphed to become a linchpin practice of contemporary American subject-formation in all kinds of other arenas (especially American politics, as we shall see); and that mass authenticity logic has ironically come down to us through the counterculture of American folk, rock, punk, rap, and other forms of popular music. As Keir Keightley notes, "One of the great ironies of the second half of the twentieth century is that while rock [popular music broadly conceived] has involved millions of people buying a mass-marketed, standardized commodity (CD, cassette, LP) that is available virtually everywhere, these purchases have produced intense feelings of freedom, rebellion, marginality, oppositionality, uniqueness and authenticity."[5]

The twentieth century was an era that, to borrow some terminology from Michel Foucault, saw a decisive shift in the individual's relation to the social whole, a shift that Foucault diagnoses as the movement from a society of "discipline" to one of "biopower," a distinction that we can initially translate like this: discipline functions within and depends on a Fordist understanding of factory society (where the individual is understood as a cog within the larger social machine, and thereby has a series of disciplinary roles to fulfill—daughter, student, doctor, patient, tinker, tailor, soldier, spy). Contrast that with the laissez faire, neoliberal consumer society in which we presently live (where everyone's primary job is to become yourself, we hope without external intrusion by the government), and you can see how the disciplinary idea of fitting in within a larger social whole (or merely working on the assembly line of the social, for the greater good of all) is now looked upon as dangerous, totalitarian, un-American even. In a world where everything is filtered through an individual's life or lifestyle (rather than through larger disciplinary questions about configuring an optimal social cohesion), biopower has become the dominant logic: everything in a society of biopower gets filtered through the lens of the individual subject. And the American individual in the twentieth century, and into the twenty-first, learned how to become a subject in large part from popular music and its logics of authenticity, which as Keightley reminds us are centrally concerned with harnessing "distinctive individualism as the key defense against the alienation of mass society."[6]

1

Biopower Blues

In Foucault's career there is a well-known shift between his work on disciplinary institutions and power (culminating in *Discipline and Punish* [1975], an exhaustive history of the prison as the central institution of disciplinary power) and his late work on sexuality, wherein he introduces a mutation in modes of modern power. According to Foucault, a new form called biopower (with its primary operating system of sexuality) is born in nineteenth-century Europe and gradually becomes dominant in the twentieth. While we will eventually delve more deeply into this mutation from discipline to biopower, just to begin with the most obvious opening example, think of the shifts in Western economic production over the past one hundred years or so from a factory economy of discipline (everyone trained to master his or her segment of the mass-production process) to the supposedly creative capitalism of our day (which is all about individual empowerment and niche markets: lifestyles, innovation, creativity, and identity). Today the dominant mode of economic production entails producing any given person's life and lifestyle, not mass-producing identical objects; in fact, niche-market consumption is oftentimes ideally refined to a market of one: "Welcome to Amazon.com, Jeffrey. We have some suggestions for you." Lifestyle purchasing is the primary economic driver in a neoliberal finance economy, and that form of hyperconsumption is dependent on constant biopolitical innovation. (This, for example, explains why China is relocating masses of its population, around 250 million people, from the rural countryside into prefab cities: to unleash the power of the Chinese consumer.)[1]

As I intimate above, popular music has had a linchpin place in shifting emphasis from a society of rigid disciplinary training to an aspirational society of individual lifestyle goals and desires. In 1976 Vacláv Havel summed up the global distinctions between a dominant discipline and an emergent biopower in terms of Western rock music, or more precisely, in terms of the Communist regime's attempts to ban rock music in Eastern Europe. What you see in that drama of the repressive state versus popular music, as Havel writes, is not "two differing political forces or conceptions, but two differing conceptions of life. On the one hand, there was the sterile Puritanism of the post-totalitarian establishment and, on the other hand, unknown young people who wanted no more than to be able to live within the truth, to play the music they enjoyed, to sing songs that were relevant to their lives, and to live freely in dignity and partnership."[2]

Here Havel lays out concisely the biopolitical importance of popular music within a disciplinary framework: pop music's function is not merely entertainment. Rather, listening to popular music goes all the way into the tall grass surrounding differing conceptions of "life" itself: whether life is all about doing your disciplinary part for the greater good of the state and the authorities (society understood as an assembly line, each with his or her own job in the factory that is the nation) or whether your individual rights to happiness and freedom trump everything else—a biopolitical world where all people would be allowed and even encouraged to "sing the songs that were relevant to their lives." Music's role in this gradual and uneven shift from discipline to biopower likewise helps explain why American parents over the twentieth century have been dependably out-raged by the supposedly profligate qualities of popular music shifts throughout the years: jazz, swing, crooners, bebop, rock 'n' roll, soul, punk, disco, rap, grunge, and hip-hop. Each of these new movements was received with suspicion precisely because popular music consumption is heavily associated with an indi-vidualist, identity-based, biopolitical economy ("doing your own thing," as they used to say) and a concomitant shift away from the disciplinary imperatives of getting with the program: from discipline to biopower.

In his lecture courses touching on the concept of biopower (*Society Must Be Defended* and *The Birth of Biopolitics*), Foucault discusses the ways in which an emergent biopower might differ from the disciplinary mode of power (which aims at modifying individual behaviors and is always mediated through institu-tions). As Foucault explains in his 1975–76 lecture course *Society Must Be Defended*, biopower comprises

> a new technology of power, but this time it is not disciplinary. This technology of power does not exclude the former, does not exclude disciplinary technology, but it does dovetail into it, integrate it, modify it to some extent, and above all, use it by sort of infiltrating it, embedding itself in existing dis-ciplinary techniques. This new technique does not simply do away with the disciplinary technique, because it exists at a different level, on a different scale, and because it has a different bearing area, and makes use of very different instru-ments. Unlike discipline, which is addressed to bodies, the new non-disciplinary power is applied not to man-as-body but to the living man, to man-as-living-being.[3]

As Foucault insists, this new form of biopolitical power doesn't simply replace discipline but extends and intensifies the reach and scope of power's effects by freeing them from the disciplinary focus on "man-as-body" through the "exercise" of training carried out within various institutions.

Biopower, one might say, radically expands the scale of power's sway: by moving beyond discipline's "retail" emphasis on training individual bodies at linked institutional sites (family, school, church, army, factory, hospital), biopower enables an additional kind of "wholesale" saturation of power effects, distributing these effects throughout the entire social field. What Foucault calls this "different scale" and much larger "bearing area" for the practices of power make it possible for biopower to produce more continuous effects, because one's whole life (one's identity, sexuality, diet, health) is saturated by power's effects rather than power relying upon particular training functions carried out in the discontinuous domain of X or Y institution (dealing with health in the clinic, diet at the supermarket and the farm, sexuality in the family and at the nightclub, and so on). Hence, biopower works primarily to extend and intensify the reach of power's effects: not everyone has a shared disciplinary or institutional identity (as a soldier, mother, nurse, student, or politician), but everyone does have an investment in biopolitical categories like sexuality, health, or quality of life—our own, as well as our community's.

Discipline forged an enabling link between subjective aptitude and docility: as Foucault concisely puts it in *Discipline and Punish*, the disciplinary body becomes "more obedient as it becomes more useful."[4] For its part, biopower forges an analogous enabling link, but this time between the individual's life and the workings of the socius: one might say we become more "obedient" to neoliberal, biopolitical imperatives the more we become ourselves, insofar as the only thing that we as biopolitical subjects have in common is that we're all individuals, charged with the task of creating and maintaining our lives. And that biopower-saturated task is performed not solely at scattered institutional sites (as it was for discipline) but virtually everywhere, all the time, across the entirety of our lives. That being the case, the major difference between discipline and biopower is that in a biopolitical society, power no longer primarily has what we might call a "mediated" relation that is aimed at confining or rigidly defining individuals (which is to say, power is not primarily doled out through institutional training as much as it is a question of direct access to one's life or lifestyle). Foucault describes the biopolitical society as a world "in which the field is left open to fluctuating processes, . . . in which action is brought to bear on the rules of the game rather than on the players, and finally in which there is an environmental type of intervention instead of the internal subjugation of individuals."[5] The bearing area of disciplinary power is what you can do, and it's primarily invested in training at a series of institutional sites. Through a kind of intensification of discipline, the bearing area of biopower has morphed into your entire life—even your taste in music—and thereby biopower's relation to any given individual tends to be less mediated by institutional factors and instead constitutes a more "environmental," diffuse, and engulfing (one might even call it "ambient") form of power.

Transversally connected to this shift in dominant modes of power, the role of music—popular or otherwise—mutates in the transition from the disciplinary society of institutional training to a biopolitical society of identity. A disciplinary society composes itself through a series of linked and segmented institutional enclosures: those sites of graduated training conjured in the Godfathers' great song, "Birth, School, Work, Death." Idealized middle-class American teenagers of my era, for example, would wake up in the family home and, after eating a bowl of sugary cereal poured from a box featuring a tiger or a leprechaun, ride the bus to school, where all day they'd get training in the disciplines of reading, writing, and arithmetic, alongside more subtle but pervasive training in social hierarchy and obedience to authority. Then they'd go to their after-school job or sports-team practice (more training, more authority) before finally returning home to watch three networks of largely awful and identical television programming, one-third of which was composed of advertisements (a different kind of training, to be sure, but discipline nonetheless). They'd do their homework (the disciplinary apparatus of schoolwork intersecting with the disciplinary apparatus of the home) and then repeat it all the next day.

In such a world, at least as this disciplinary subject experienced it, popular music played a largely resistant role: while the world of popular music circa the late 1970s was in retrospect training of a sort (in hip consumerism, in taste-making, in negotiating a social "scene"), music collecting and listening was nevertheless largely something that happened in the interstices of everyday life's institutional, disciplinary compulsions. You couldn't listen to Led Zeppelin alongside your institutional training—not at school, at work, or at baseball practice. And even listening at home entailed headphones plugged into the stereo because my parents hated that stuff. Listening to popular music in the disciplinary era tended, in other words, to take you out of the enclosed economies of disciplinary training and give you a certain amount of time to yourself, or at least gave you a respite from the drudgeries of a seemingly nonstop series of disciplinary architectures and tasks. In your room, at a party, in the car, in the interval spaces between institutions—that's where music could function against the grain, offering at least a momentary buffer: the raised fist of a Bruce Springsteen tune, the funky soul of James Brown, the girl power of the Runaways, or the wallowing negativity of Pink Floyd. Surely there was music out there within the institutions of the disciplinary world (at the grocery store or mall, at work, or on the AM car radio in the form of jingles written for commercials), but that music largely included sugary pop tunes and neo-Muzak, designed to assuage (rather than to explore or intensify) the very feelings of anger, isolation, and anxiety inevitably drummed up by the enclosures of the disciplinary society.

Fast-forward to the biopolitical society of today, where on a recent trip to the grocery store I heard Bad Company's "Can't Get Enough of Your Love" playing over the sounds of wobbling shopping cart wheels. And this was at the downscale grocery in town. (At the more upscale Wegmans, I recently heard the National's "Fake Empire"—"We're half-awake / in a fake empire"—which is a song explicitly designed to intensify feelings of isolation and anxiety and thereby one would think a poor accompaniment to choosing between the Oreos and the Hydrox.) And it's not just at the grocery store. In a surprising turn (at least it's very surprising to me), during the decades since my disciplinary childhood, the antidisciplinary popular music of my youth (now rebranded as "classic rock") has become the Muzak of our day, to be heard everywhere from the dentist's office and the home-repair store all the way to TV and radio advertisements for any product you can imagine. Indeed, while up-tempo ditties and sincere smiles were advertising's bread and butter in the disciplinary society (sunny housewives crooning, "Don't cook tonight / call Chicken Delight"), in the biopolitical society you can hardly move a product without a rebellious rock soundtrack coupled with an ironic wink and a nod. For example, Kentucky Fried Chicken somewhat oddly used classic-rock staple "Sweet Home Alabama" as its theme song in a 2005–6 ad campaign (odd because it's not *Alabama* Fried Chicken, but perhaps Neil Diamond's "Kentucky Woman" was unavailable for use). Clearly, the Colonel wanted to use the song to highlight his chicken's rebellious streak and its proud southern heritage, even if Alabama is not exactly Kentucky.

And while the rise of disco, punk, new wave, grunge, hip-hop, indie, and rap since the 1970s did much to change the *sound* of the sixties-inspired rock canon, each of these musical formations, at some level, merely built on the antidisciplinary "me versus the Man" *logic* of 1960s and '70s popular music—the importance of being your own person, flipping the boss the bird, taking it to the streets, having fun, saying it loud. And this antinomian "personal authenticity" stance of popular music fans has become, for better or worse, the official house style of American biopolitical capitalism in the twenty-first century.

When it comes to linking the logic of biopower with the logic of popular music, the connection is perhaps nowhere more succinctly stated than in David Hesmondhalgh's *Why Music Matters*. He offers this concise response to his titling query:

> The fact that music matters so much to so many people may derive from two contrasting yet complementary dimensions of musical experience in modern societies. The first is that *music often feels intensely and emotionally linked to the private self* . . . music is a set of cultural practices that have come to be intricately bound up with the realm of the personal and the subjective. . . . The second is that *music is often the basis of collective, public experiences*, whether in live performance, mad dancing at a party, or simply by virtue of the fact that thousands and sometimes millions of people can come to know the same sounds and performers.[6]

Much against the grain of his own highly optimistic humanist premises (the book argues that music matters because it helps facilitate what Hesmondhalgh calls "human flourishing," a phenomenon that one might less generously dub the "great extinction event that is the Anthropocene"), he does at least make it clear why music matters to a world where biopower is the dominant mode of power: if biopower strives to connect individual lives and identities seamlessly to mass demographic patterns, then we can see more easily music's privileged status as a kind of operating system for biopower. Music "matters," as Hesmondhalgh so clearly shows us, because it's a set of intimately and deeply personal investments, yet at the same time it's a mass social phenomenon. In any case, that's the biopolitical magic: "Music, then, represents a remarkable meeting point of intimate and social realms. It provides a basis for self-identity (this is who I am, this is who I'm not) and collective identity (this is who we are, this is who we're not), often in the same moment."[7] Insofar as "music's seemingly special link to emotions and feelings makes it an especially powerful site for the bringing together of private and public experience,"[8] that fact likewise makes music a privileged operator within a regime of biopower. In his essay on "Music and Identity," Simon Frith restates the biopolitical claim succinctly: "Identity is not a thing but a process—an experiential process which is most vividly grasped as *music*. Music seems to be a key to identity because it offers, so intensely, a sense of both self and others, of the subjective in the collective."[9]

2

Steal Your Face

There is no better way to illustrate the difference between a society of discipline and one of biopower than by looking at the reception of popular music in the twentieth century. Specifically, I'd like to call attention to a 1967 CBS special report (available on YouTube) hosted by the aptly named Harry Reasoner, where American viewers were warned about a growing youth menace in San Francisco, "The Hippie Temptation" (the temptation there being the hippie lifestyle of sex, drugs, and rock 'n' roll).[1] Reasoner's prime examples for this special report were (who else?) the Grateful Dead, who are seen sitting around their Haight-Ashbury commune house smoking cigarettes (and God knows what else), playing songs, and talking peace, love, and mind expansion—with the middle-aged CBS guy in a suit playing the straight-man heavy with real verve. I encourage you to watch the whole clip on YouTube, but I'd like to begin by zeroing in on the moment when the interviewer asks the Dead what they hope to accomplish by nonparticipation in mainstream social life as we knew it in the 1960s. Why not get with the disciplinary society? Get a job, get married, start a family, grow up, dammit! Various members of the Dead reply by insisting they don't want to "accomplish" anything—they just want to live free from interference by the Man, which will of course later become the mass-individualizing mantra of biopolitics. As Reasoner notes, the hippies exemplified by the Dead "do not want" the existing disciplinary identities (worker, family member, citizen, soldier) that "our civilization" offers them, "except on their own terms"; they recognize the immense problems of society, but "their remedy is to withdraw into private satisfactions," which Reasoner concludes is the "greatest waste of all." The whole thing is pretty funny, in retrospect, and it even reminds us that Jerry Garcia didn't always have a beard. (I'd always assumed he was born with one.)[2]

But what's most peculiar about "The Hippie Temptation" is that its tone and demeanor—disciplinary power wagging its fingers at people who want only to be left alone to self-actualize—looks like something completely foreign to the American present, even though it was only a half century ago. If nothing else, watching the show today makes it crystal clear that the hippies, and their biopolitical sense that all revolution starts with and moves through the revolution of the individual, won the American culture war decisively. In the neoliberal world of radical, just-do-it individualism, all but gone are the imperatives of Reasoner's disciplinary world, where we're each supposed to sit down, shut up, and do our jobs for the greater glory of society. (Even the U.S. military, which would seem the last bastion of this kind of disciplinary thinking, sells itself these days as a biopolitical self-actualization technique: "An Army of One.")

Today, we have all succumbed to "The Hippie Temptation"—which is to say, our social world is no longer centered on docile, disciplined individuals working at their assigned roles to ensure more cohesive social wholes. Rather, we live in a biopolitical world of what Gilles Deleuze calls control, where constant innovation, resilience, and disruption are the mantras du jour—where the modulating part is the constantly morphing whole and vice versa. We've all transformed into what Deleuze has dubbed the constantly modulating "dividual," rather than the in-dividual segmented and molded by discipline.³ As Margaret Thatcher so elegantly put it in 1979, for neoliberal biopower "there's no such thing as society. There are . . . men and women and there are families. And no government can do anything except through people, and people must look after themselves first. It is our duty to look after ourselves and then, also, to look after our neighbours."⁴ Translated into Ronald Reagan's American idiom, the individualist sirens' song of neoliberalism goes like this: "Government is not the solution to our problems. Government is the problem."⁵ Likewise, if the fluid mutations of constantly updated lifestyles are the basic unit of everything for a biopower-based society, then neoliberal consumption capitalism is the logical organizing principle or operating system for this discontinuous mass of dividuals, held together only by their quests to become who they really are, ceaselessly following Dead drummer Bill Kreutzmann's biopolitical prescription in "The Hippie Temptation": always be "expanding your consciousness, changing your life." That biopolitical sentiment translated a decade later into Thatcher's refrain that it "is our duty to look after ourselves." Or as the Dead starkly lay out the premises of biopower (the journey of the self as walking the path of life between the "dawn" and "the dark of night"), no one can finally share your experiences because "That path is for your steps alone."⁶

Neoliberal consumption capitalism finally makes only one product: subjects, dividuals, selves. This is what Maurizio Lazzarato calls (following Félix Guattari) the "machinic enslavement" of subjects to neoliberalism—enslavement here not signaling its disciplinary function, people subjectified or confined to a specific identity and forced to work as a cog in a machine of the social, but signaling our contemporary biopolitical "enslavement" to the project of endlessly creating our own identities and subjectivities.⁷ Pindar's ancient wish—that we could all live by the dictum "Become who you are"—has morphed, as Lazzarato and Guattari suggest, into our contemporary biopolitical compulsion.[8] And of course, it's not only the Grateful Dead "driving that train / high on cocaine." Just think of the near state-funeral level of grief afforded in 2016 to biopolitical music pioneers David Bowie and Prince—both of whom showed us how to be ourselves by imitating world-famous media superstars who are mutating constantly, always following their creative desires into uncharted subjective territory.

And while "enslavement" to this project of constant self-creation is perhaps an inflammatory term (Lazzarato suggests the word enslavement is synonymous with Foucault's "government," which is only to say we're worked on constantly by regimes of power that impel us to become ourselves), it is true that we really don't have any "choice" in the matter. The only salable commodity of the neoliberal present is your subjectivity, which is under constant reconstruction, deconstruction, and modification by the machinic forces of capitalism. As Guattari puts it, "Essentially, capitalism depends on asignifying machines."[9] As Deleuze helpfully adds, these days "the self does not undergo modifications; it is itself a modification."[10]

So maybe the hardest thing to reconstruct looking back at "The Hippie Temptation" is why anybody thought the hippie menace was something worth worrying about in the first place—any more than the dangers of jazz (now rebranded as "America's classical music"), punk (the Clash song "Pressure Drop" played under a 2007 commercial for the Nissan Rogue and "Should I Stay or Should I Go" served as the 2016 jingle for Choice Hotels), or even hip-hop (which is now the official soundtrack of the affluent white suburbs) were in their respective days. While these musical-social formations were of course perceived as dangerous at their moments of emergence, it's harder to remember that from the vantage point of the biopolitical present, because the danger posed by hippie music only makes sense within a disciplinary society (where rampant do-your-own-thing-ism was a social problem or a "temptation"—as opposed to today, where such self-obsession is the iron rule). As discipline becomes a residual formation and biopower ascends to the position of a cultural dominant, the function of cultural formations like popular music also changes drastically: within a generation, the directive "Just Do It!" morphs from a slogan or practice challenging disciplinary norms (for example, when it serves as the title of Jerry Rubin's 1970 hippie manifesto) to an imperative that functions as an axiomatic confirmation of control society's biopolitical dictates (as in its reinvention as Nike Inc.'s official slogan). And subjective authenticity is thereby hoist on this petard of biopower precisely because within a disciplinary apparatus, authenticity suggests individual subjectivity operating as a norm-busting transgression of the normative social dictates. In a biopolitical society, however, subjectivity as norm-busting transgression is the norm and rule, so the contemporary function of authenticity discourse—musical or otherwise—is largely left to push against an open door.

In short, the mutating landscape of twentieth-century popular music has coincided with the rise of biopower and the triumph of neoliberal society (wherein questions of individual subjective identity are directly connected to larger demographic shifts, a system where all we have in common is that we're all continuously trying to sculpt and modify our lives). Now surely other twentieth-century art forms found themselves saturated with biopower, economics, and technology as well (say, novels and poetry with individual readers and the publishing industry; drama with the economics of patrons and falling demographics for live theater; visual art with galleries and museums, and so on). But popular music has far deeper saturation into the socius (for example, a lot more people listen to music every day than read literature on a daily basis). However widespread popular music listening may be (one of the reasons why it's a privileged linch-pin for understanding recent cultural production), in the end I'm just as interested in the residual disciplinary authenticity-logic that's remained so central to popular music practices. Of course, novels or poetry or film also depend on a certain kind of authenticity discourse. Any given person doesn't just read anything or go to see any old film; subjects choose (if that's the right word) according to a certain kind of authenticity logic: you like historical novels or experimental poetry, while I like action films or romantic comedies.

To channel Pierre Bourdieu for a moment, the subjective uses and functions of all art forms depend to some degree on a mediating logic of "taste," and taste is a category of discrimination based largely on the logic of authenticity and scarcity. As Bourdieu argues, in sizing up artistic practices, nothing offers *social* distinction to a subject more than the way a person makes *cultural* distinctions among aesthetic objects or practices. And of course, popular music practices (of production, consumption, and circulation) are where this logic is most intensely on display and where the logic of "mass authenticity" has to do a certain kind of heavy lifting in taking a ubiquitous commodity like popular music and making it a cornerstone of a very personal, individual identity statement. As Bourdieu insists in *Distinction: A Social Critique of the Judgment of Taste*, "nothing more infallibly classifies than tastes in music."[11] And it is precisely this biopolitical work—individual subjectivity sculpted on a mass demographic scale, with the two intertwined in a single set of practices—that makes popular music a singularly rich site for analyzing neoliberal society.

3

Not for Sale

When our old friends the Grateful Dead played their final "Fare Thee Well" concerts over the Fourth of July weekend in 2015, there was predictable grumbling from many Deadheads: the whole thing was a sellout, a cash grab, and a betrayal of the wandering roadshow ethos that had made the band a counterculture icon for nearly half a century. For many of the faithful, the Dead were maybe the last vestiges of the "old, weird America" that Jerry Garcia conjured when he suggested that in the late twentieth century, you could no longer plausibly run away to join the circus, but you could satisfy your wanderlust by following the Grateful Dead through a year of shows. Throughout the 1970s and '80s, the Dead offered a steady diet of such shows, which in turn offered Deadheads around nine months per year of camping out, hitching rides, selling T-shirts and acid, trading tapes of shows, and living below the radar of the taxman and the local cops. The Dead played a whole lot of concerts over those years, while they didn't really sell all that many records; and this in turn earned them additional underground cultural capital as "anticommodification" icons—in it for the authentic love of the music and the community, not the money.

Though of course there was always the other side of that coin, the sort of stuff that makes for books like Barry Barnes's

Everything I Know About Business I Learned from the Grateful Dead:
the Dead were authentic all right, but they were also routinely
among the highest-grossing acts in any given year well through
the 1970s and '80s (because record sales tended only to make
record companies rich, not necessarily the bands themselves).
In fact, the Dead are now seen as avatars of the new media
economy of shareware: they boldly gave away their content for
free (not only encouraging but facilitating fans' taping of their
live shows), and thereby the Dead solidified the authenticity of
their brand with a fiercely loyal customer base. Whatever else
they may have been, the Dead's decades as a traveling roadshow
also constituted a long, strange, graduate economics seminar in
cross-platform niche marketing ("Do you like Dancing Bear LSD
and bootleg cassettes of that killer 1977 Cornell show? Maybe
you'd be interested in these tie-dye drapes for your VW micro-
bus.") So the question remained hovering over those final shows:
were the Grateful Dead authentic artists taking a final bow . . . or
money-grubbing sellouts milking fans for all they were worth?

Thus is reconfigured yet again the "way cool/sold out" dialectic that I've suggested is symptomatic of so many discussions
concerning popular music. Is Kanye West really "Not for Sale,"
as his logo proudly pronounced during his 2013 performance
on *Saturday Night Live*? Or is the anticommodification "Not for
Sale" stance simply a position you have to espouse if you want
to be successful within the current landscape of popular music?
When that discussion stalls (either Kanye is for sale or he isn't
for sale), then we can move on to endless similar discussions
around and about musical authenticity—about my having liked
Daft Punk before they went mainstream and became famous,
or your insisting that the world has come to an end because
you can hear Alabama Shakes playing behind an Apple computer TV commercial, Iggy Pop's "Lust for Life" being used to
hawk luxury cruises ("that's like hypnotizing chickens"), indie

rocker Sharon Van Etten's music featured in both luxury auto commercials and ads for undrinkable beer (Volvo and Corona), or a Taco Bell spot featuring Joe Jackson's "One More Time" (conjuring his song "I'm the Man" and its biting refrain "I can sell you anything"). Or vice versa, you could argue that it's the height of authenticity for artists (or their estates) to take control of their songbooks and do whatever they want with them: why *wouldn't* a Ramones' song be featured in a TV ad for a pricey Peloton home-workout bike? And I think I heard somewhere that 2Pac loved Sprite, so it makes sense to use his music in the background of a soda commercial. As I type this sentence listening to internet radio, I just heard a DJ on Minneapolis's fine indie station "The Current" revealing that he had no idea who the Buzzcocks were until he heard their music in a 1999 Honda commercial. Given that Metallica was featured in a 2016 Dodge ad, I hope new generations will discover their music as well. Some say that the commercialization of formerly authentic music is the end of the world—everyone has sold out. Others say it's the birth of a brave new world—who wouldn't want to hear something good, rather than something crappy, playing in a restaurant or in a TV ad? Round and round we go.

In any case, this "way cool/sold out" dialectic is undoubtedly another one of the myriad things that Grossberg was referencing when he complained that nothing much had changed in the last half century of critical writing about popular music. Wander into virtually any bar around happy hour this Friday, and you can strike up this kind of authenticity conversation in a nanosecond. Insofar as I'm looking to move beyond the sort of things that people routinely say about popular music, I somewhat ironically want to insist on—rather than try to apologize for—popular music's overdetermined status within such a commodity culture. And I'd also like to put "authenticity" to bed as a critical or theoretical model in talking about music. The seeming centrality of musical authenticity is, as I've already suggested, one of the primary reasons why writing about music has become so hopelessly stalled and repetitive: you say it's authentic, I say it's sold-out crap. Music of course can and does produce meaningful cultural authenticity-effects for its listeners and producers, but you'll never find this representational thing called authenticity "in" any music. Likewise, the jargon of authenticity may have deployed a certain capacity for resistance in a disciplinary society (allowing one perhaps to stand outside the normalizing dictates of a Fordist factory society—we used to call it "waving your freak flag"). But the mass authenticity compulsion of biopolitics offers very little friction to a post-Fordist, neoliberal control society, where we are all compelled endlessly to stand outside normative dictates and constantly modulate our subjectivity.

In the end, popular music fans are less autonomous, taste-making, deciding subjects than they are dividual relays within a series of much wider flows—for example, flows of money, desire, and technological innovation. Neither anticommodity nor simply "sold out," the discourse surrounding popular music is on the contrary a key factor in understanding how a whole matrix of practices can produce those authenticity-effects, so often associated with being "not for sale," inside a wholly commodified context. Producing and maintaining this wonderfully oxymoronic mass-produced authentic individualism has been the primary cultural "work" of popular music over the past half century.

As such, the discourses and practices surrounding popular music production and consumption over the past few decades offer a skeleton key to understanding a larger shared American (indeed, increasingly global) phenomenon: the biopolitical importance of mass authenticity—the kind of thing that seventy thousand people at the final Grateful Dead concert share with the demographically distinct throngs at Coachella or Bonnaroo, not to mention those who attend the Big Barrel Country Music Festival, the ESSENCE or Jazz & Heritage festivals in New Orleans, the Alive Christian Music Festival, the season at Tanglewood, Festival Latino, the Full Terror Assault gathering of metal-heads, the Michigan Womyn's Music Festival, or the Brooklyn Hip-Hop Festival. Obviously, the demographic makeup of these audiences (in terms of race, ethnicity, class, age, gender, religion, sexual orientation) are widely disparate, but the biopolitical phenomenon of "mass authenticity," accruing so powerfully to popular music discourses and practices, stitches these categories all together into a larger "logic," one that will help us to understand how subject production and reproduction works—how it operates—in the biopolitical era of neoliberalism.

Of course, one could always argue, as Joseph Heath and Andrew Potter do in their *Nation of Rebels: Why Counterculture Became Consumer Culture*, that late twentieth-century American counterculture, and especially its soundtrack, never offered any kind of meaningful resistance to American capitalism. They argue that counterculture could hardly be "co-opted" or "sold out" because it was never in opposition to the economic mainstream values of American capitalist society to begin with:

> There simply never was any tension between the counterculture ideas that informed the '60s rebellion and the ideological requirements of the capitalist system. While there is no doubt that a *cultural* conflict developed between the members of the counterculture and the defenders of the older American Protestant establishment, there was never any tension between the *values* of the counterculture and the functional requirements of the capitalist economic system. The counterculture was, from its very inception, intensely

entrepreneurial. It reflected . . . the most authentic spirit of capitalism.[1]

While this argument tracks in some ways parallel to my own, especially in its attempts to end-run around talk of "co-optation," I'm keen to make a distinction from them: for Heath and Potter, capitalism seems not to have changed at all over the past decades, and thereby capitalism's "ideological requirements" have always-already been neoliberal or biopolitical, "intensely entrepreneurial" at their core. However, I'm arguing that such widespread emphasis on biopolitical entrepreneurship was demonstrably *not* the case for American capitalism in its mid-century disciplinary or Fordist phase. Before the biopolitical, neoliberal revolutions of the Reagan-Thatcher 1980s, disciplinary capitalism didn't have much use for subjective authenticity. Having worked at a gum factory as a summer job in the late 1970s, I can attest that no one encouraged us to think of ourselves as entrepreneurs or rebels, nor were we implored to innovate anything at all on the assembly line. Disciplinary systems, as Foucault insists, want to fix subjects into certain molded roles in order to assure the efficient production and reproduction of goods and services.

With the development and triumph of biopolitical capitalism, on the other hand, the question of value always needs to be run through the individual, and I'm sure that gum factory employees these days (the few who haven't been replaced by robots) are constantly called upon to innovate, share best practices, think outside the box, and parrot all the other noxious clichés of neoliberalism. But my point here is this: *American popular music's values of subjective rebellion and personal authenticity were not always coincident with the logic of mainstream American economic life.* (Indeed, as we shall see in the next section, musical "authenticity" itself has a thorny history of rise and fall in the twentieth century.) In short, popular music's countercultural notions of personal authenticity as resistance to massification did perform an immense amount of useful work at the tail end of the disciplinary society in America: if the problem is subjective constraint, doing your own thing registers quite nicely as resistance. However, if several decades later the axioms of neoliberal capitalism dictate that you must be your own entrepreneur, that sense of sixties-style personal authenticity can only confirm, rather than contest, the normative practices of American economic life. In short, it's not that popular music sold out to the Man, or that musical rebellion and authenticity were always already a shill for the Man; rather, my argument is that the dominant logic of American capitalism has morphed into a biopolitical form that was presaged by twentieth-century American popular music fandom and its intense investment in developing and maintaining your own personal authenticity within a wholly commodified field.

4

A Genealogy of Popular Music and Authenticity; or, You *Can* Fake the Funk

The discourse surrounding popular music and authenticity is yet another one of those things that seems like it hasn't changed much over the past half century: figures as diverse as Billie Holiday, Roy Orbison, and Biggie Smalls are equally revered for the authenticity of their respective musical accomplishments. We should begin, I suppose, by stating the obvious: the question of musical authenticity only becomes a hot topic within a world of mediated, technologically reproducible music. In short, musical authenticity only becomes a question in a historical epoch wherein music has already become a technologically reproducible commodity. In the nineteenth century, when the only way you could hear music was live, the question of its authenticity would be largely nonsensical, because musical authenticity (at least as we came to understand the word in the twentieth century) presupposes some kind of relation between an authentic original and a fallen or second-rate copy. In a world where there's only live music, you could certainly argue over better or worse composers and performers of music, or more or less stirring renditions of particular songs, but the question of musical authenticity as we understand it today would hardly apply in a world where there are only "originals," here-and-now live renditions of a song.

The twentieth-century question about authenticity is perhaps best thematized by Walter Benjamin in his 1930s essays on "The Work of Art in the Age of Its Technological Reproducibility." In previous historical epochs, Benjamin reminds us, the experience of any art form was singular, rare, and rooted in a particular context. The relation to art brought about in the viewer an *Echtheit*, a "thisness," that undergirded the artistic experience. You could only hear music or experience drama live, unfolding in real time at a unique, singular place, and as such, the glow of aesthetic experience was both rare and precious. Such was what Benjamin famously calls the "aura" of art in the era before mass reproducibility, that "something-more-than-the-everyday" that accompanies the overwhelming aesthetic experience of an original artwork.

But as works become infinitely reproducible, artistic aura inevitably fades, or at least aura has to be produced differently in a world where everyone has seen a picture of the Mona Lisa or heard Mozart on the car radio. In fact, aura not only fades, but it actually inverts in an era of technological reproducibility. In my experience, for example, students who've actually seen the Mona Lisa report not overwhelming artistic aura but a kind of disappointment: "It's small, faded, old, I had to wait in line for an hour to see it when I've seen it a thousand times before," and so forth. On a more personal register, I remember the first time I saw a suite of paintings by Vermeer in Amsterdam and, despite myself, my primary affect was shock at how *small* they are. I'd seen hundreds of reproductions of various sizes and had always assumed the originals were quite large. At Benjamin's historical juncture, when modes of artistic perception change due to technological advances, the question of artistic authenticity—let's follow Benjamin and call it the problem of technologically reproducible aura—inexorably becomes transformed alongside the emergence of film, radio, photography, and the phonograph.

The authenticity conversation within twentieth-century American popular music configures itself within the realm of commercially reproduced music and really gets off the ground with considerations of jazz in the 1920s and '30s. To continue stating the obvious, we should note that the question of American popular music's authenticity is inexorably bound up with considerations of race from the get-go. As Amiri Baraka points out in his 1963 classic *Blues People*, the authenticity discourse of twentieth-century American popular music centers squarely on African American traditions, housed in stories as oft-repeated as Bix Beiderbecke visiting black clubs in the 1920s and Benny Goodman paying for Fletcher Henderson arrangements, through Elvis's first hit in the fifties (covering Big Mama Thornton's version of "Hound Dog"), and the first meeting of Mick Jagger and Keith Richards (who each recognized the African American blues records the other teen was carrying), all the way to hip-hop white kids in the twenty-first-century suburbs fetishizing the "street" experience of urban people of color. In short, the question of race has been tightly imbricated with the question of popular music authenticity in America. Long before Jackie Robinson and Bill Russell became famous and admired as authentic American sports heroes, black musicians were welcomed into mainstream America's heart (my mother's favorite singer was Nat King Cole, who was also a great piano player—check out the Lester Young Trio sides); though African American musicians were certainly not welcomed into mainstream America's neighborhoods, nor its most venerable artistic institutions, at least not through the front door.

It's easy enough to explain this link between musical authenticity and the black experience in terms of outright theft by mainstream American culture: first the theft of black bodies and labor in the slavery of the seventeenth through nineteenth centuries, then the stealing and repackaging of black music in the twentieth (swing, blues, and rock 'n' roll), all the way through the theft of black experience itself in the mainstreaming of twenty-first-century hip-hop and rap. And that theft from African American culture surely and plainly has been the case: as the disciplinary apparatus of the nineteenth and early twentieth centuries gave way to the biopower of our identity-based era, so too we see a change in what moneyed mainstream culture needs to harvest from black lives. Those needs shift from the brutal agricultural slavery of the colonial period through the nineteenth century, to the Chicago or Detroit disciplinary factory jobs of the northern migration in the twentieth century, to the mainstreaming and massification of biopolitical questions concerning individual authenticity, marginality, struggle, and identity in the twenty-first. As Shannon Winnubst argues in *Way Too Cool: Selling Out Race and Ethics*, it was a mainstream commodification of "cool" that biopolitical neoliberalism lifted from black culture in the mid- to late twentieth century. As Winnubst puts it, "When neoliberal markets sell 'coolness,' they are not only bastardizing nonconformity into a hollowed-out, generic posture; they are also commodifying black resistance in the process. As an aesthetic that originates in US black culture, 'cool' offers resistance and rebellion through access to 'something better.' This racialized character of 'something better' . . . marks black culture as both alluring and dangerous in the white imaginary. But as coolness is gradually co-opted . . . into contemporary white, consumer-class aesthetics of hipster rebellion, it becomes commodified."[1] However accurate this analysis proves, the theft of a commodified, deracinated notion of "cool" from black culture ultimately begs a prior question: How or why does African American music become a privileged site of authenticity to be exploited by mainstream American culture in the first place, as the United States negotiates the shift from disciplinary to biopolitical capitalism? How does the small, seemingly marginal formation of African American music become the driver for almost all American popular music going forward into the rock era and beyond? How or why did we become, as Funkadelic puts it, "One Nation Under a Groove"?

According to Baraka, what mainline American culture wants and extracts from the black musical experience is not so much a notion of "cool" but what he calls the music's essence as a "verb"—an active, ongoing response to the experience of oppression. The American culture industries then take that musical verb (say, "blues" or "swing") and make it into a noun, a consumable (and supposedly universal) "experience" of modern life (of struggling, being sad, happy, frustrated, in love, whatever). So while Baraka doesn't use the Foucauldian nomenclature of discipline and biopower, his explanation of why black music drives American popular music has everything to do with the first inklings of biopower's emergence within mainstream American culture in the early and middle twentieth century. Given the experiences of existential angst that rose with the Cold War and the increased role of technology in everyday life, the musical forms of African Americans begin to look to alienated white suburbanites as authentic—rooted in some more honest or "real" experience that's more raw and truthful in its expression of joy or pain or love, or at least more inspiring than mainstream pop music like Bing Crosby or Paul Whiteman. This authenticity myth lives into the twenty-first century nowhere more intensely than in gangsta rap. As Tricia Rose puts it, "Although it's well known that mainstream commercial hip hop's obsession with black gangstas and ghetto street culture is a product line, the illusion that it is unadulterated remains."[2]

As Baraka insists, however, this is all a myth, insofar as historical African American music like the blues is not a raw or spontaneous form, but an intensely modern and mediated one that gives voice and feeling to the dangers faced by former slaves seeking home and work in a postslavery economy. In the intensification of the shift from discipline to biopower that emerges in the twentieth century, popular music—and specifically black music—offers to white Americans an "authentic" expression of the difficulties of fitting in within a context that seems hostile or foreign: the first few days of high school, the breakup with Jennifer, or the family where no one understands you. This middle- and upper-class white teen angst is of course a far cry from the brutal structural racism that gave rise to the blues tradition, but within the emergent biopolitics of the twentieth century, the native concerns of the blues tradition—Who am I and how do I fit into a place where I don't belong?—find a welcome home in white suburbia, though those concerns were of course born (and borne) by black people far from Shaker Heights, Ohio, or even farther from the record stores of London in the 1960s. As Baraka succinctly puts it, the blues tradition that gave form and life to jazz and rock 'n' roll was also the undergirding authenticity discourse that "gave a local form to a general kind of nonconformity that began to exist in American (Western) society after WW II."[3]

Black jazz musicians created something that white musicians wanted to play (because of its swing), and the music also offered a jazz attitude or stance toward what Baraka calls "the sinister vapidity of mainline American culture"—certainly what Bix Beiderbecke heard in Louis Armstrong, what the Beat poets heard in Charlie Parker, or what Van Morrison heard in Howlin' Wolf.[4] Of course, on the surface this appropriation suffers from an obvious historical amnesia concerning the "meaning" of the blues tradition. Muddy Waters's "Mannish Boy" has a very different valence for a black man from the Jim Crow South when it's originally recorded in Chicago in 1955 ("I'm a man / no b-o-y") than it does when it pops up as a macho anthem on the soundtrack for Martin Scorsese's Italian-mobster drama

Goodfellas in 1990. But for Baraka, the disconnect (or the assimilationist connections, depending on your point of view) between white hipsters and black musicians is also a question of differing identities, different returns on the investment in a counterculture stance. As Baraka writes, "The white beboppers of the forties were as removed from the society as Negroes, but as a matter of choice. The important idea here is that the white musicians and other young whites who associated themselves with this Negro music identified the Negro with this separation, this nonconformity, though, of course, the Negro himself had no choice. . . . Being a Negro in America, one *was* a nonconformist."[5] While white jazz players saw a subject position they could inhabit on any given Saturday night (and throw off on Sunday morning), black musicians of course could not choose to put on or take off a nonconformist position in relation to mainstream culture. And in addition, while white musicians and fans saw a rebellious stance in jazz, Baraka insists that "[Louis] Armstrong was not *rebelling* against anything with his music. In fact, his music was one of the most beautiful refinements of the Afro-American musical tradition."[6]

5

Good Rockin' Tonite

With the birth of rock 'n' roll in its breakout year of 1955, or so the story goes, the authenticity discourse that surrounded the subculture of jazz and its *players* (Bix admiring Armstrong) shifted focus to a whole series of postwar American youth *consumers* in search of some kind of personal authenticity to fight against the bland suburban conformity of the Eisenhower years. The dominant narratives we tell ourselves about the first birth of rock 'n' roll in the midfifties suggest that something new, authentic, and highly meaningful burst onto the scene when Elvis Presley cut a few sides in Memphis and from there went on to change the world.

As Greil Marcus spins out the story in *Mystery Train*, early rock 'n' roll was "authentically new as any music can be":[1] "It was an explosion, and standing over it all was Elvis. In the single year he recorded for Sam Phillips—July 1954 through July 1955—ten sides were released (four more were used by RCA to fill up Elvis's first album): about half derived from country songs, the rest took off from the blues. His music stands to the rest of rockabilly as genius does to talent."[2] From the vantage point of 1975, Marcus reckons that Elvis's "blues especially have not dated at all. Not a note is false; their excitement comes through the years intact, unburdened by cuteness, mannerism, or posturing. Nothing is stylized. The music is clean, straight, open and free."[3]

While Marcus is here clearly engaged in constructing a usable past for rock music, and those Sun sides are quite fine, we'd also have to admit that things really don't work that way—where some kind of "clean, straight, open and free" genius comes out of nowhere to change everything aesthetically, historically, or technologically speaking. And if we fast-forward more than forty years from Marcus's writing of these lines in the midseventies, it seems clear that this kind of origin-story myth-making is much more about 1975 than it is about Rock1's native moment in 1955. By the midseventies the mainstream musical innovations of the late sixties had given way to the soft-rock flatulence of Steely Dan, Jackson Browne, the Eagles, and their ilk (a kind of easy listening music sometimes derisively called "Yacht Rock"), and therefore the authenticity discourse within popular music was in need of some rejuvenation. American rock's transgressive or innovative version of authenticity and raw honesty would find this needed jolt a year later, with the advent of punk (the Ramones' first record was released in April 1976); but from the vantage point of 1975, with the Eagles' "Lyin' Eyes" all over the radio, interrupted only occasionally by Fleetwood Mac's "Say You Love Me" (with overproduced bestsellers like Browne's *Running on Empty* and Fleetwood Mac's *Rumours*, not to mention the Michael McDonald years of the Doobie Brothers, on deck to be released soon thereafter), it was clear that rock was floundering and in need of some authenticity help. And looking back to Rock1 offered critics and artists of the midseventies a template for songs "unburdened by cuteness, mannerism, or posturing," like the music of Elvis that supposedly gave authentic birth to rock in 1955.

As any number of critics and sociologists have pointed out, the myths of American postwar teen rebellion at the birth of rock in the midfifties are largely nonsensical.[4] The first baby boomers would still have been in primary school in 1955. Given that the boom didn't really get off the ground until the early fifties, most of those baby boomers would in fact have been in diapers, not in need of a rebellious music to stick it to the woody station wagons and repressive high-school principals that haunt our collective imagination concerning the 1950s—the myth of a simpler time, when transgression was real but harmless. Of course, that mythology surrounding 1950s America was largely constructed as a palliative for the post-Watergate 1970s. Beginning with George Lucas's film *American Graffiti* (1973) and its morphing into the long-running television sitcom *Happy Days* (1974–84), the 1950s became a sort of field where all kinds of people in the 1970s (on both the ideological right and the left) went hunting for a kind of authenticity.

However, as Elijah Wald points out in *How the Beatles Destroyed Rock 'n' Roll*, Elvis Presley (or most any other rocker of the 1950s) didn't understand what he was doing to be an authentic, bold new expression of transgressive aesthetic purity (whatever that would have been). Rather, Elvis understood what he was doing as of a piece with the dominant musical practices and discourses of the time: Elvis admired Perry Como and Frank Sinatra and seems very much to have thought of himself as an entertainer rather than a visionary genius or breakthrough artist. Just look at Elvis's reaction to the scandal surrounding his first television performance on the *Milton Berle Show* in June 1956. If you look today at the YouTube clip of that performance (of "Hound Dog"), you can still see what all the fuss was about and why Elvis and early rock 'n' roll were as much visual as sonic phenomena, creatures of television and its variety show format of the 1950s as much as they were products of the radio and record industry.[5] Elvis does some suggestive hip thrusting during the performance, but in a bit of very gutsy bravado, he closes with a slow, mic-stand-grinding routine under a very extended bawdy recitation of the song's lyrics. It was sexy to be sure, provocative undoubtedly, the stuff upon which legends are built.

That performance on the Berle show immediately got Elvis banned from the biggest taste-making TV show of them all in the 1950s, the *Ed Sullivan Show*, which would have spelled trouble for his developing career as a potential heartthrob movie star. So what did the rebel Elvis do several weeks later when he got a reprieve and landed on Sullivan's major rival, the *Steve Allen Show*? Well, he definitively did *not* do what later artists like Courtney Love or Elvis Costello or Chuck D would likely have done (doubled down on some even more outrageous performance, solidifying their rebellious street cred). Rather, Presley agreed to don a tuxedo and repeat his performance of "Hound Dog," this time singing it to an actual dog, a baggy-faced basset hound that Steve Allen brings on to the stage.[6] Watch this as well on YouTube and you'll see a sheepish Elvis who pets the dog, mugs with it, and nuzzles the hound a few times; the whole thing borders on cute and is certainly surreal. But one thing it's not is *authentic*, if we take that word in its modern musical sense of dripping with rebellious, innovative artistic integrity. Here, Elvis is clearly trying to get back into the good graces of the mainstream public—essentially apologizing for his performance on the Berle show in the hopes of making it to the Promised Land: Ed Sullivan's soundstage.

At the time Sullivan was having none of it, and his July 1, 1956, show had booked a tribute to Hollywood director John Huston on the same night Presley was on the rival Steve Allen program, singing to a pooch. Up against Elvis, Sullivan offered a litany of Hollywood royalty testifying to the greatness of Huston, the highlight being Gregory Peck offering dramatic readings from *Moby-Dick*, the topic of Huston's then-latest film. However compelling that sounds, the Steve Allen program, like a ratings version of Melville's white whale, decisively sunk Sullivan's show for the evening. In retrospect that's not very surprising, as Elvis was a hot commodity, and people were dying to tune in to see what he was going to do next. (And this incident offers decisive anecdotal evidence, if there is such an oxymoronic thing, that popular music trumps literature and film as a strange attractor for mass cultural influence—today for sure, but even in the 1950s.)

And Elvis's act of contrition, alongside his ratings triumph, on the *Steve Allen Show* did its job: it got Elvis his first gig several weeks later (in September 1956) on the Sullivan program, where he also performed a tamer version of "Hound Dog" and a few other numbers. Sullivan was not in the theater that night, still recovering from a car accident, but suffice it to say that Elvis was a hit, and he appeared two more times in the coming months. Elvis in fact closed the Sullivan show on his final appearance, in January 1957, with the a cappella gospel song "Peace in the Valley," clearly designed and performed to reassure older viewers and parents that Elvis was not a sex maniac or smut peddler.[7] Sullivan introduces the gospel number as the kind of thing that Elvis really cares about; in fact, according to Sullivan, it represents "the mood he'd like to create" with his music. After the song, Sullivan hurries over to Elvis to heap praises on him as a truly humble young man, one of the best people he's ever had on the show. Sullivan specifically says, "I want to say to Elvis Presley and the country that this is a real decent, fine boy." Sullivan concludes by offering his showbiz blessing to Elvis, "You're thoroughly all right." Mission accomplished, Berle show transgression mopped up, off to (lucrative, but aesthetically dubious) Hollywood stardom goes Elvis.

Through the late fifties and early sixties Presley is likewise doomed to some years in the wilderness musically, only really to be reinvented as a singer after the advent of Rock2, in his

1968 comeback special (which sees him decked out in a black leather outfit, retroactively birthing the mythology of his mid-fifties "authenticity" creds). That "rebel" Elvis is of course born only *after* the counterculture success of the Rolling Stones, the Doors, or Jimi Hendrix, but back in the fifties Elvis hardly understood what he was doing as counter to anything about American life, much less as anything artistically "authentic." As Elvis put it in 1956, "I like to sing ballads the way Eddie Fisher does and the way Perry Como does. But the way I'm singing now is what makes the money. Would you change if you was me?"[8]

In fact, the discourse surrounding fans' attraction to artistic authenticity and American popular music really began not with rock in the 1950s, but with folk music that became popular (though nowhere near on the same scale) in its wake. In the fifties rock is largely a continuation of business as usual, reading out of the playbook authored for the crooners and the swing phenomenon (largely consisting of repackaging African American forms for the entertainment of white suburban audiences). In fact, the folk revival of the late fifties and early 1960s constituted a direct rebellion against the commodified nature of Rock1 and its disposable, top-forty star system. And thereby folk music, playing somewhat against its typecasting as people's music, largely introduces this exclusivist question of authenticity into the discussions about American popular music fandom. As we saw with Baraka, authenticity was clearly an operative concept among jazz musicians well before the 1960s, but the question of authenticity is largely if not wholly absent from the early rock lexicon in the 1950s: if music is or remains a form of "entertainment," the question of its authenticity is largely moot. If you're entertained by it, fine. It's not required that entertainment be authentic. As Keightley writes, "during the 1950s, rock 'n' roll was regularly viewed as just one in a series of passing dance crazes, giving way to the calypso and the twist. . . . Even rock 'n' roll performers themselves might have scoffed at the idea that they were doing anything more than entertaining their audiences."[9]

With folk music, however, is born the sense that mass popular music is or can be more than (mere) entertainment, more than just a commodity to be consumed. Rather, allegiance to a certain kind of music could put on offer not just a temporary mood to be enjoyed but a full-fledged identity position to inhabit. Folk introduces into the American landscape the idea that your taste in popular music can and does matter personally or politically, *even for people who don't play instruments*. Again, a discourse of authenticity was already familiar in the 1940s and '50s to jazz-producing musicians—jazz drummer Buddy Rich, for example, thought Elvis was a total square.[10] But this authenticity discourse was not so much in use among music consumers, people who went out dancing to swing bands. The major shift introduced by folk music is the switch to the fans beginning to see some sense of identity in the music, or the fact that the music takes on or provides "meaning" in fans' lives. It's not Elvis's swiveling hips but Pete Seeger's banjo that Marcus should be lauding as the twentieth century's musical authenticity breakthrough.

As Frith explains, the Rock2 music of the mid- to late 1960s depended for its ideological commitments not on the Rock1 of the mid-1950s but on a refashioned version of folk music's bedrock commitments to authenticity. As Frith explains, 1960s and '70s

> rock is *used* by its listeners as a folk music—it articulates communal values, comments on shared social problems. The argument, in other words, is about subcultures rather than music-making; the question of *how* music comes to represent its listeners is begged. . . . For the rock ideologues of the 1960s—musicians, critics and fans alike—rock 'n' roll's

status as a folk music was what differentiated it from routine pop; it was as a folk music that rock could claim a distinctive political and artistic edge.[11]

If Elvis did not really see what he was doing as existing at a far remove from (much less a form of resistance against) the "routine pop" of the era, certainly Seeger or Joan Baez *did* understand what they were doing as a reaction to the commodified sounds of the radio hit parade. So with folk music is born many of the primary imperatives of musical authenticity discourse going forward through the twentieth century and into the twenty-first: the music is to be taken seriously; it's not merely entertainment or distraction; and there's a potential series of identity positions (for both individuals and larger communities) embedded not only in *playing* the songs but, just as importantly, in being a *fan* of such music. In short, folk music is the first mainstream popular music that *matters* for its listeners as something significantly more than entertainment. And here fan authenticity emerges on the American music scene, to be taken up from folk into Rock2 (with some important changes, as we will see). But as Frith insists, it's folk music (not Rock1 or Elvis) that enabled and nourished the ideology of late 1960s Rock2 fans: "Armed with this [folk] ideology it was easy enough for 1960s rock fans to hear their music as more authentic than pop too; to claim that even if their music was commercial, it nevertheless symbolised a community."[12]

It's this commitment to "community" that is most decisively retooled in the shift from folk to Rock2 in the 1960s, because the folk community and the performer's seriousness have an actual referent within the folk music scene: a leftist commitment to celebrating the working class songs and lives of the dust bowl and fighting against discrimination in the Jim Crow South. Even if folk singers wrote their own songs, their performances were designed not to showcase and profit from their individual artistic genius but to conjure and mobilize a sense of community. Singers were conduits for a common experience of the people, not visionaries to be admired for their aesthetic genius. (Though we should note that these folk songs had no penetration within the actual communities they valorized. Frith points out that no Woody Guthrie songs were found among the Oakies and Arkies who went west in the dustbowl migrations, for example; they already listened to the hit parade on the radio. In fact, folk music actually represented a community composed almost entirely of young, white, leftist college students and urban bohemians.)[13]

All that changed, however, in the early 1960s, most obviously with Bob Dylan, who caused an authenticity stir in the folk community when he "went electric." Which is of course a stir caused less by his embracing technology (folk music was amplified for years before) than his embracing the "rock" sound and style and thus turning his back on the folk vision of authentic commitment to community and making a play toward becoming a commodified "star." Dylan would turn in the midsixties toward producing hits and thereby becoming someone who reveled in his own world rather than using his songs to provide an occasion for the folk community to come together and advance its collective causes.

Here in the Rock2 shift of the mid-1960s, the folk ideology of authenticity is kept alive, but in an inverted fashion: from the midsixties on, performers are more authentic the more they are dedicated to following out their own artistic vision. When someone from the audience yells "Judas" at the electric Dylan near the end of his 1966 tour (as we see preserved on film at the conclusion of Martin Scorcese's *No Direction Home*), Dylan calls him a "liar" and turns to his band, saying "Play it fucking loud!" while he gives the finger to the Judas guy from the stage. To those of us who grew up in the Rock2 world and after, this Dylan "fuck you" moment (rather than his renditions of a sincere acoustic political song like "Blowin' in the Wind") is Dylan at his most authentic (perhaps on the heels of his electric "Maggie's Farm" performed at the 1965 Newport Folk Festival, a similar middle finger offered to the folk music establishment). It seems more authentic because here we see Dylan throwing off the shackles of being a representative of this or that movement or ideology and following his own visionary path. As Frith writes, in the middle 1960s mass musical authenticity is retooled through inversion (rather than scrapped outright): "it was this notion of authenticity—truth to experience rather than to class or organisation—that the 1960s folk performers retained as they became rock singer-song-writers. They combined the folk conventions of sincerity with literary devices drawn from beat poetry; their 'authenticity' was the result of a combination of soul-baring and poetic vision. . . . The paradox of rock ideology in the 1960s was that performers' claims to represent a community (unlike the usual 'plastic' pop singers) were supported by the marks of their individuality."[14]

Here in the transition from folk to Rock2, from the community's values to the individual's vision as the primary thing that fans value or have in common, popular music discourse enters a distinctly biopolitical authenticity labyrinth from which we have not yet emerged. Not only Rock2, but the ensuing mass popular music movements of punk, disco, grunge, hip-hop, and rap have all continued to depend (in one way or another) on this notion of authenticity as the artist's personal vision and genius correctly indexed to the sincerity, originality, and realness of the life portrayed in the music. Rock2 authenticity says "no" to constraint and follows its own vision. And the resulting community is an ironic biopolitical community of individuals, each dedicated to following out his or her own authentic desires—authentic in this case not because they reflect a folk vision of unity but precisely because each of us has in common that deeply personal striving to become who we really are. And who better than a rock star (a Jim Morrison or a Mick Jagger) to represent that kind of uncompromising individuality to which we all aspire?[15]

6

Musical Community, from In- to Excorporation

As Grossberg develops it, the authenticity discourse within the Rock2 formation of fans and users depends on "excorporation," which is to say it depends on saying "no" to some very specific things (rather than authenticity resting in saying "yes" to some very specific things, as in the folk version of authenticity). As Grossberg succinctly puts it, the apparatus of popular music fans is "affective (rather than ideological)" (driven by feelings and largely a-rational investments rather than consistent aesthetic or political positions); and thereby the logic of investing in X or Y popular music is less unifying than it is "differentiating (us versus them without providing necessary content to the 'us')."[1] As Grossberg lays it out, the logic of rock music authenticity within everyday life has been driven not by positive content (say, agreement on a specific canon—rock guitarist Ronnie Montrose is in, Pat Travers is out) but by opposition to particular targets (boy and girl bands, "top forty," anything autotuned or overproduced, bands where musicians don't play their own instruments or write their own songs, and so on). What makes the rock authenticity formation so powerful is that it can produce its authenticity effects entirely by negation, rather than by agreement on or dedication to some clumsy core content. As Bourdieu phrases this premise in more general terms, "Tastes (i.e., manifested preferences) are the practical affirmation of inevitable difference. It is no accident that, when they have to be justified, they are asserted purely negatively, by the refusal of other tastes. In matters of taste, more than anywhere else, all determination is negation; and tastes are perhaps first and foremost distastes, disgust provoked by horror or visceral intolerance ('sick-making') of the tastes of others."[2]

Indeed, negation is the primary driver of the whole modern musical authenticity configuration and helps explain why people can argue endlessly about the relative merits of particular bands or albums both outside of and within their own musical formulation. It's easy enough to "excorporate" Justin Bieber or Taylor Swift (too popular, too bubble-gum, not authentic), but the "productive no" of the rock authenticity formation allows substantial (even endless) jockeying within the rock formation itself. For example, is so-called southern rock really rock, outside of the Allman Brothers and Lynyrd Skynyrd? Are the Red Hot Chili Peppers a great band, or do they suck? How much punk or grunge is really just rock? What about rap, which Jerry Garcia infamously dismissed as "not music" because the genre consists largely of vocals—which he derisively characterizes as "talking"—backed by samples from other songs with few original instrumentals? It might be poetry, Garcia grudgingly admitted, but it's not music.[3] In any case, it's this highly productive "no" that characterizes the Rock2 musical authenticity practice, and it depends decisively on discrimination within and outside of a category, not on any hard and fast agreement on positive content (insofar as that would be more kowtowing to "the stifling Man," no?). Rock authenticity, in the end, is not necessarily to be found in saying yes to Neil Young, Janis Joplin, and Jimi Hendrix; rather, it's to be found in saying no to Captain & Tennille, Engelbert Humperdinck, and the Starland Vocal Band.

In retrospect, the apparatus surrounding popular music fandom in the late twentieth century was never so much grounded by agreement concerning the *great* songs or artists but by a consensus concerning what the *shitty* songs or artists were. People who like rock music, for example, can disagree about the relative merits of Aerosmith, while rap fans can argue East Coast versus West Coast all day, because what binds these musical formations together is not finally positive content of some kind but mutual loathing for some other kinds of music. Popular music fandom encompasses a flexible identity logic because it doesn't depend on each of us within the fan group liking each and every one of the same things (for every two rock fans who love the Beatles, there's one who hates them). For musical authenticity, so much depends on each and every one of us disliking the same things—say, Rod Stewart's disco phase or the late work of Phil Collins. As an aside, I'd note that those rock fans who dislike the Beatles tend to do so largely because they thematize the Beatles as a bubble-gum pop group—see "I Want to Hold Your Hand," for example—who later got pretentions to artistic authenticity when it became fashionable, if not necessary to continued sales, to morph into visionary "artists" offering up supposedly "revolutionary" sentiments within Hallmark-card-ready artistic drivel like "All You Need Is Love." In any case, the question that interests us here is not whether the Beatles were any "good" or not, but how the discourse surrounding popular music can function to attract and assign such deeply felt personal commitment to a wholly mass-produced product like the Beatles. The question is, how and why does it make any difference whether anyone thinks the Beatles are any good or not? And the answer is the "mass authenticity" logic of excorporation, one that allows me to be different from everybody else by investing in a mass-produced commodity like rock, rap, country, or indie—different forms that, as Keightley reminds us, are related in that each is a "massively popular anti-mass music."[4]

This excorporative practice has in turn allowed popular music's logic of authenticity to travel far and wide from its home turf (music-related arguments) and seep into the groundwater of twenty-first-century American biopolitical subjectivity—where any given subject's authenticity is no longer to be found positively "in" X or Y practice, person, or formation but in a subject's dislike for W or Z practice, person, or formation. Take, for example, American politics—where both the Left and the Right are these days driven not so much by positive content or widely shared values but by a blind hatred for the other side. Especially in the Far Right wing of American politics, you can see this contentless excorporation logic of authenticity functioning in an almost pure way: they're against government regulation, handouts, universal health care, taxes, immigrants, the Koran, and so forth. But what are right-wing politicians *for*, or what is the positive content of their message? Who knows, but it doesn't really matter, because their authenticity is purchased not by adopting and espousing any kind of common positive dogma but by saying "no" to a common series of things. Here you build community not through positive ascribing to the same core disciplinary message or values but through sharing your strong dislikes (how someone like the thrice-divorced womanizer Trump managed to court the religious right in 2016: "At least he's not Hillary," the saying went). And this excorporative practice has in turn allowed the discourse of rock authenticity to extend beyond its origin (music-related arguments of the classic rock era) and become the overarching logic of twenty-first-century American biopolitical subjectivity. This contentless sense of authenticity has become the primary biopolitical territory of contemporary American subject-formation, one that has ironically come down to us through the late twentieth-century counterculture of American rock, rap, punk, and other mass alternative musics.

It is probably punk music that most obviously picks up and runs with Rock2's excorporation or negation thesis. As Marcus puts it in *Lipstick Traces*, punk "used rock and roll as a weapon against itself."[5] One only has to think of the Sex Pistols' enduring catchphrase ("No Future") or watch their brilliant closing cover of Iggy Pop's "No Fun" at their final performance in San Francisco in 1978 (droning over and over, "No fun / no fun / This is no fun") to see punk music doubling down on the negating function of Rock2. Insofar as the authentic refusal of rock excorporation first and foremost works to create a kind of subcultural identity by denigrating mainstream tastes, punk was the obvious successor, rather than antagonist, to the classic rock era. Punk's performers negated mainstream values with constant sneering glee.

Of course, the dominant culture being negated in punk (which is to say, the economic situation in the United States and Britain in the late seventies) is quite different from the economic and cultural situation of the late sixties. By 1980 neoliberalism, and its reaction to the economic and cultural "excesses" of the 1960s, was in the process of being installed by Margaret Thatcher in the UK and by Ronald Reagan's election in the United States. As Marcus points out, punk rock's negation works largely to dramatize this historical situation at the dawn of every-man-for-himself neoliberalism and the parallel commodification of everything, even—maybe especially—authentic oppositional or subcultural identity. The totalizing negative critique is perhaps best summed up by Johnny Rotten's last words as a Sex Pistol, spoken before the mic drop that closes their final show: "Do you ever feel like you've been cheated?"[6]

Punk rock, in other words, constitutes a sort of postmodern moment of reflexivity concerning the relation between music and authenticity itself (a move that literature or painting had experienced a generation earlier—calling the whole artistic project into question, from Andy Warhol's questioning the distinction between art and commodity through his endless iterations of soup cans and Brillo boxes to Amiri Baraka's exhorting us, in his poem "Black Art," to "fuck poems").[7] In retrospect, then, punk rock is less a critique or transgression of the Rock2 ethos than it is a cry for the exhaustion of rock authenticity as a form of opposition to supposedly mainstream social values: perhaps the sixties didn't die at Altamont but at CBGB in the 1980s. Punk rock names the moment where there is no outside anymore: we're all inside the machine. But here we also see very starkly drawn the limit of the negation authenticity thesis: Can you really say no to everything? Including yourself and your friends? This was in fact the dream, and punk rock intensifies the logic of negation to its phoenix point; but punk can't sustain this project, really, insofar as the relentless deconstruction of everything is not a sustainable undertaking. With punk rock, Marcus suggests, music becomes a performance art project, akin to Dadaism or the postmodernism of the highly reflexive novel (Ishmael Reed, Thomas Pynchon, David Foster Wallace), endlessly pulling the rug out from under itself. And avant-garde art projects are largely doomed as mass drivers of identity formation.

Economically speaking, with the triumph of neoliberalism, the logic of subculture in America has become the whole of culture, and thereby rock music's excorporative "no" to mainstream culture has become itself mainstream. Neoliberal American culture from Reagan forward is largely driven by a series of contentless negations, which can only function as politically progressive in an era where there is such a thing as a stifling mainstream culture, musically or otherwise—a mainstream decided by the radio, the record companies, or more generally by the taste-making controllers of the culture industry. Fast-forward a half century, and none of those mainstream gatekeepers exist anymore, or where they exist, they really don't exert all that much top-down cultural influence. Just look at how wrong the *New York Times* got the 2016 election of Donald Trump, or how little of what's left of the music industry could see viral internet sensations like Danger Mouse's *The Grey Album* or K-pop sensations like "Gangnam Style" coming—or even how little mainstream culture brokers could see rap coming in the late 1980s, when N.W.A.'s breakout album *Straight Outta Compton* sold two million copies without any backing from any of the normative musical outlets of the day (MTV, radio stations, hit parades).

And this adopting of negation as the house style of American neoliberalism is clearly signaled and presaged by the logic of popular music—in, for example, the way that punk rock became "alternative rock" in the 1990s precisely as this gesture of refusing mainstream American culture became mainstream itself.[8] Or just think of the parallel political rebranding we've seen in right-wing American politics over the past several decades, from the Moral Majority of the 1980s (which desperately wanted to be seen as a mainstream, or a forgotten one) through the Tea Party individualism of the 2010s, all the way to the rebranding of old-fashioned white nationalism as the Alt-Right movement in the Trump era: these days, even Nazi sympathizers want to brand themselves as "alternative," authentic individualists saying no to mainstream culture. In each of these contentless refusals, it's the position of "maverick" that gets traction politically. In the era of neoliberal individualism, nobody (Right or Left) wants to be branded as mainstream anything, and the cultural and political logic of that mass refusal of the mainstream was honed far from twenty-first-century politics in the rock authenticity years of the late twentieth century.

Punk's intensification of Rock2's decisive "no" could perform dependably undermining political work only in a world of solid social norms and easily identifiable mainstream aesthetic tastes, a world increasingly we only know from films about "sticking it to the Man" in the 1950s to 1970s. From the sixties through the dawn of the punk era, it may well be that subcultural style and meanings had the power to subvert the commitment to wholeness and consensus valued by the mainstream; this at least is the extended thesis of Dick Hebdige's 1979 *Subculture: The Meaning of Style*, where he argues that punk is dedicated to "the subversion of common sense, the collapse of prevalent logical categories and oppositions . . . and the celebration of the abnormal and the forbidden."[9] Punk's thoroughgoing "opposition to dominant definitions"[10] is, for Hebdige, "intrinsically subversive"[11] insofar as punk seeks to "substitute the values of 'fissure' and contradiction for the preoccupation with 'wholeness'."[12]

Hebdige's description of the subversive role of punk music in late disciplinary society makes sense in terms of its own era (the mid- to late 1970s), but if we fast-forward to today, we begin to see that the constant undermining of social consensus, the dedication to fissure and subversion, or even the fact that "punk style is in a constant state of assemblage" no longer functions against the day of American-style neoliberal capitalism.[13] Subcultural subversion of the mainstream is out of a job when we reach a historical point where mainline American culture is made up of nothing but a bunch of subcultures, each offering its differentiating "no" to other subcultures. (One thinks here of the endless comic headlines after Donald Trump's election: "Americans All Agree: Country Hopelessly Divided.") Certainly for music in the twenty-first century, the rapid triumph of the MP3 stream or download, and the volume of music it's made available on the internet, has rendered taste-making institutions like mainstream radio, record stores and record critics, or MTV almost wholly obsolete when it comes to producing a culturally dominant taste or sound. Record companies no longer try to form consumer taste by signing what they take to be potentially hot acts, to record and publicize these acts to make them famous and profitable; today the (remaining) big labels largely wait for some act or artist or song to go viral on the internet, and then they sign those acts to recording contracts to cash in on their already wild popularity.

It is in turn this against-the-mainstream version of the now-mainstream authenticity logic in the twenty-first century that leads to Grossberg's "disappointment" in the subversive potentials of popular music and popular music criticism. The solidarity-creating "no" of rock identity formation (the baby boomer generation's "no" to the values of their parents' generation, a kind of solidarity by subcultural negation) doesn't any longer function in a largely progressive fashion: it's the logic of the Far Right as much as it is the logic of the hipster Left, as Naomi Klein ironically signals in her double-negative book title *No Is Not Enough*. But negation's inverted functionality is due not to the fact that authentic subcultural nay-saying has been co-opted or ripped off by dominant culture, but rather because the terrain of so-called dominant culture has shifted under neoliberal capitalism, from a Fordist or Cold War "us/them" logic of a privileged mainstream hoping to defend itself against subcultural incursions, to a world where the mainstream is nothing other than a large bundle of niched subcultures. In the absence of a stifling, norm-driven "do what you're told" mainstream, rock identity's "no"—what Marcus conjures when he insists that "negation is always political"—cannot produce an "oppositional" political identity.[14] The gesture of negation remains the same, but the terrain on which that gesture operates has changed radically such that the "no" functions everywhere, in a thousand different subcultures, and allows us to enjoy such formerly oxymoronic sights as heroin-addicted murderer Sid

Vicious endorsing luxury sedans (an Acura TV ad featured Sid's cover of Sinatra's biopower anthem, "My Way") or Chance the Rapper in a Kit Kat commercial. In a world of mainstream neoliberalism, rock authenticity's "do your own thing" has become the law of the whole—even if "your thing" is being in a commercial for a candy bar.

Which is to restate in somewhat different lingo something that I argued above: rock's authenticity-producing "no" (without any necessary "yes" or core content) has migrated from its position as a musical identity marker to become the dominant form of identity configuration in the American present. From the Trump campaign to academic discussions of "performative identity" to Sprite soda imploring you to "Trust your gut, not some actor" (all formations with very different political valences, targets, and effects), the thing that seems important is that the logic of identity practice (excorporation without a norm) is largely homologous in all these cases, and that logic was forged and battle tested in and around the fan discourse surrounding popular music since the 1960s. It may be that we in the United States no longer have citizens (little bundles of rights and responsibilities), but we live in something more like a highly developed fan culture surrounding our politics. The name that Benjamin gave to the flowering of such a culture in the 1930s in Germany is well known and chilling: the a-rational enthusiasms of fascism, a social formation that consistently aims at the "*aestheticizing of political life*."[15] Even Deleuze and Guattari, for whom "music is never tragic; music is joy," nevertheless recall for us "the potential fascism of music."[16] For his part Bourdieu likewise reminds us of music's intense a-rationality: "Art is also a 'bodily thing,' and music, the most 'pure' and 'spiritual' of the arts, is perhaps simply the most corporeal . . . an experience deeply rooted in the body."[17]

It's worth noting at this juncture that such bodily a-rationality can function in a progressive mode politically, as Barry Shank argues at convincing length in *The Political Force of Musical Beauty*. Given all our Bourdieu-style musical disagreements, or the inverse fact that people from very different political orientations can profess to enjoy the same music (Paul Ryan, for example, is a big Led Zeppelin fan), Shank asks how musical experience can lead to any kind of political community. "Simple: political community is not characterized by sameness. A political community does not consist of those who agree on the matters at hand, but instead is made up of those who recognize each other as speaking with legitimate political voices."[18] "Simply put," Shank continues, "the political force of music derives from its capacity to combine relations of difference into experiences of beauty,"[19] a future-oriented and collective musical sense of aesthetics that is importantly different from those exclusivist identity-confirming experiences of "meaning." While this seems very persuasive to me as an ontological argument (the open space of bodily experience provoked by music keeps the political future open to discussion and contestation), it's Shank's neo-Habermasian hope that we "recognize each other as speaking with legitimate political voices" which seems to me in short supply these days. I really don't see that kind of recognition and respect on offer when hip-hop fans talk about country music or vice versa—and even less so when the pundits on Fox News begin talking about MSNBC or vice versa.

And Shank recognizes this divisive side of dissensus when he notes in his conclusion: "There is no necessary political trajectory that results from musical listening."[20] Nevertheless, music's political force for Shank rests in a constant reminder of the common, open space of the political, the being-in-common or political-aesthetic project of sense-making that we all share. In fact, Shank shares my concern with troubling the logic of authenticity in musical discussions because he sees authenticity as the primary place where the originary openness of musical experience gets closed down, where the deconstructive experience of the future-to-come slides into an inflexible insistence on the status quo. In theoretical terms Shank sees invocations of musical authenticity as the place where the political force of music turns away from evoking Jean-Luc Nancy's welcoming community of dissensus toward Carl Schmitt's rigid political thinking based on the centrality of the friend-enemy distinction. Indeed, Shank recognizes this political force of musical affect could go in Schmitt's highly divisive "us versus them" direction just as surely as it could gesture toward an open, common experience of "beauty": "Rock's desire for authenticity, a consequence of the genre's emergence in the era of mass culture combined with its ambitions to achieve art status, can result in a drive for purity that mimics Schmitt's exclusionist [friend versus enemy] concept of the political. More than a mere formal homology, rock's insistence on an exclusive grasp of the authentic generated a distribution of the sensible that marked all other genres as either meaningless mass entertainment or nonsensical noise—as insufficiently significant to matter politically."[21] This exclusionary banishment of others (and their tastes in music) constitutes the dark side of authenticity's "excorporative" functioning.

And by invoking fascism and Schmitt (who was the preferred political theorist of the Third Reich), I'm not trying to suggest that all pop music fans are neofascists; however, it is true, as any discussion about the relative merits of Beyoncé or Springsteen will show you, that in general fans aren't known for their inclusive, well-reasoned views, but for their gut feelings on the matter at hand. Fans know automatically what's authentic and what's not, and no amount of exposure to Rascal Flatts or Big & Rich is going to convince hardcore indie-rock fans that new country is just as important or valid as Father John Misty's music (just as no amount of discussion in 2016 could bring Donald Trump voters around to voting for Hillary Clinton or vice versa). In any case the point is this: wherever it may function, a biopolitical logic of fan authenticity trends inexorably away from consensus or a cohesive social order. Take it from me—I saw more than one fistfight in my high school years over whether *Wish You Were Here* was a great Pink Floyd album or a piece of shit. Keightley explains the stakes of such adolescent scuffles: "Even as there is a basic, underlying agreement between the various versions of rock that *some* form of authenticity is required to distinguish rock from the corruption of the mainstream, there may be polemical disagreement over what form it should take. Often these distinctions are deployed to divide cultural spaces that are otherwise homogeneous—say, a white, middle-class suburb—so that the minute details over which rock fans argue obsessively may become the only apparent source of individual differences."[22]

As we've seen, such a notion of fan or consumer authenticity—as defending the performer's commitment to an artistic project—didn't much function in 1950s youth culture, though it had functioned among musicians within jazz circles before that. Authenticity became a mass oppositional force against the commodification and alienation of modern life in the folk music of the 1960s, with the songs themselves offering a sense of group identity and historical roots to their legions of listeners. In the midsixties Dylan becomes the linchpin figure for taking that version of authenticity as opposition to the mainstream and personalizing it—the artist's own personal vision becomes the underwriter of authenticity. And that version of individual artistic authenticity, as a kind of visionary genius, in turn becomes the logic of a kind of "mass individuality" in the era of neoliberalism.

You can see this logic very intensely on display in a 2006 appearance by Ray Davies on Austin City Limits (available on YouTube), where he performs a version of his Kinks' 1966 classic,

"I'm Not Like Everybody Else."[23] It is of course a great song, with a memorable hook (and there's a killer cover by American garage rockers the Chocolate Watchband that in fact first introduced me to the song, and is I think better than the original). In any case, when Davies gets to the song's refrain, there's a particularly instructive camera cut to the audience, and it captures the moment that gives this book its title. When the song's titling chorus returns, the hipster "Keep Austin Weird" audience is shown, all in unison, chanting "I'm Not Like Everybody Else." Looking almost like a mini Nuremburg rally celebrating biopower, that image cements the mass individuality logic of biopolitics in one concise screenshot: I'm ironically just like everybody else in and through my axiomatic self-assurance that I'm *not* like everybody else. There's no necessary positive content for the "I"; rather, identity remains defined by the negation of "everybody else." As Keightley reminds us, popular music authenticity would have us be first and foremost "concern[ed] with finding a true self in the midst of corruption and conformity."[24] What we have in common, then, is that we're all trying to be authentic, insofar as we're all striving to do our own thing in the face of the (now, virtually nonexistent) cultural hegemony of various squares, norms, and buzzkills. And we most intensely recognize this collective individuality through our tastes in popular music.

Punk music rebelled against this kind of smug, self-assured groupthink within arena rock, but in doing so punk also continued this mass authenticity logic and in fact intensified or reenergized it (as evidenced by the fact that the Chocolate Watchband's cover of "I'm Not Like Everybody Else" was a staple reference point of the psychedelic revival in early eighties punk). However, given the fact that punk's native historical moment, global neoliberalism, found itself dedicated to the individual consumer, against the socialist groupthink of the government, that was the end for rock's ability to perform inherently progressive or oppositional political work. In short, punk's negation was a big fat "no" to a series of stifling "thems" (the norms, the suits, the junk for sale at the mall) that were already on their hegemonic way out. With the Pink Floyd fistfights a thing of the disciplinary musical past and poptimism the reigning musical paradigm today, the negating function of rock excorporation no longer lives as intensely in musical discourse; but as I've argued throughout, this negating fan logic surely does give us a skeleton key to the larger logic of twenty-first-century American biopolitical subjectivity, where at least politically speaking, "no" is about all there is.

Musical authenticity does of course continue to function in the present, at least in the discursive realm of talking about music. "Keeping it real" is, arguably, more important than it's ever been for today's emo, rap, and hip-hop. These are very different musical forms, of course, but the importance of authenticity is what ties together figures as diverse as hyper-emo singer Justin Vernon from Bon Iver and rapper Snoop Dogg: each has a deep personal (and highly race-segregated) backstory of authenticity related to their music—Snoop as a gang member in Long Beach and Compton and Bon Iver's Vernon as a tortured soul living and recording alone in a cabin in northwest Wisconsin. So although musical authenticity for fans has no real referent or agreed-upon positive content (or more accurately, *because* musical authenticity has no real referent or agreed-upon positive content), it continues to function crucially far outside its birth and flowering in the popular music of the 1960s—both in popular music and in the larger biopolitical realm of everyday American life, which has become obsessed with ways to sculpt an individual authentic identity inside a mass consumer society. And the popular music authenticity logic born in the 1960s was designed to do precisely that.

Indeed, Foucault's analysis of biopower shows us how and why subjective authenticity functions in biopolitical society less as a liberation than as a trap, or a liberation that contains traps galore: we are sutured to the social in and through our most "subjective" investments (intense personal commitments like our sexuality or our tastes in music). In a biopolitical society our deepest interior states constitute a dense transfer point for social power, insofar as individuals and identities are the decisive pivots or handles for neoliberal capitalism. This, I guess, seems depressing to people (or at least it always seems depressing to my students when we read Foucault): social power goes all the way down in the viscera of my most intimate personal investments, so how can I possibly resist it? How can I be me authentically when that pivot of subjective authenticity constitutes the most intense way that I'm tethered to sinister neoliberal imperatives? But I think Foucault shows us how that is the most liberating knowledge of all. We are all connected, rather than disconnected, by our everyday struggles with power, in a constant jujitsu series of pivots toward and away from power. This, after all, is basic Foucault: where there is power, there is resistance. Capitalism works on us at the level of visceral refrains (no one has to "convince" you to consume stuff—there is no alternative), so the terrain of resistance is everywhere also the terrain of power. The question then becomes less how to "fight the power" wholesale (through the "no" of excorporative subjectivity) than trying constantly to harness (one might even say "tune") those resistances. At the end of the day, identity is a verb, not a noun; we are made subjects by actions, and we can be unmade or remade by actions as well: it's not what you think that's important, it's what you do. It's not a matter of lament or celebration of subject formation within the present regime of biopower, but a matter of searching for new tools to understand the past, present, and maybe the future of the relations between you and me and the advanced capitalism that we live with every day.

And music constitutes one such powerful social tool, as a template for understanding how biopolitical subjectivity has emerged, how it works in the present, or how it might work differently in the future: no longer as something that primarily provides meaning or an identity for any given subject but perhaps as something that provides a soundtrack for movement, a provocation to action (or inaction, if that's what you need for your cool-down mix). Music is today an operating system for everyday life rather than a template for understanding who we are deep down, really or authentically. Music provides a micrological series of functionalities in biopolitical life and thereby backgrounds the questions of authenticity, which in a world of rampant consumerism one would hope could finally be put out to pasture. There is no real you; or, more accurately, the real you is undergoing constant modification: this is neither a liberating nor a constraining realization, but it names the terrain where we live at present. Considering that biopolitical fact, any given subject today doesn't need an authentic identity to inhabit, but a soundtrack for becoming.

As the savvy reader will have noted, in forwarding this line of thinking, I'm also extending Jacques Attali's argument in *Noise: The Political Economy of Music*. Attali claims that the popular music of any given era doesn't merely *reflect* dominant economic discourses and practices but in fact *predicts* changes in economic regimes: "music is prophetic," Attali insists, and "social organization echoes it" rather than vice versa.[25] As Attali continues, music "is neither an autonomous activity nor an automatic indicator of the economic infrastructure. It is a herald, for change is inscribed in noise faster than it transforms society."[26] As we've seen, music has functioned as a herald for widespread economic and social reorganization, as in the United States we've gone from a predominantly factory society of discipline to a neoliberal society of biopower—or in Attali's terms, from a disciplinary society of endless goods-based "repetition" to what he sees in the mid-1970s as an emergent society of subjective "composition." He defines composition simply as any given individual's "production-consumption,"[27] or the (re)production of identity through consumption, what we now call the neoliberal "prosumer."

And as unlikely as the claim seems on the face of it, the practices that have sprung up around the past decades of popular music—as Attali reminds us, a powerful "mode of immaterial production"—have in fact presaged these decisive changes in the wider economy, for better or worse.[28] Music is and has been a powerful apparatus of capture for values of all kinds, but it's also a powerful tool in subverting the present and/or carving out a livable future. So where do we go from here, having arrived on the territory of neoliberal biopower that was predicted for us by the discourses and practices surrounding American popular music? It is to that question that I now turn, keeping in mind all the while Attali's clarion call (or is it a siren's song?): "Our music foretells our future. Let us lend it an ear."[29]

7

Capitalism, from Meaning to Usage

What's changed about American life over the past sixty years is less the world we live in than the territory we live on—which is maybe to say that what's changed drastically is less the idea-scape in our heads than the practices (re)configuring our everyday lives. Over the past few decades what or how people think about popular music (what it "means" to people) hasn't really changed all that much. But if you consider ways that the internet, streaming music, the MP3, the smartphone, the iPod, and the computer have decisively changed the *practices* of collecting and listening to music over recent decades, you can maybe begin to see the increasing gulf between meaning and usage. People continue to talk about music in a vocabulary not all that different from the one I learned to talk about music in the 1970s (stuff you like is authentic, real; stuff you don't like is inauthentic, fake). But the practices that configure the territory of popular music (not that long ago, collecting albums and listening to them from start to finish, or paying attention obsessively to the radio to hear your favorite song or learn about the next big thing) have been completely revolutionized. For people under the age of twenty-five, YouTube and other streaming services have become the primary source of musical discovery (not the radio, nor the record store, nor even iTunes). And through these shifting practices, we begin to see how the crucial question for thinking about popular music in the present is no longer "What does music mean?," as that's not where things have changed decisively over the last several decades. Rather, the question of the present has become "How does music function?" ("How does any given musical deployment make, remake, or unmake a territory for living—for shopping, eating, driving, dating, working out, cooling down, and so on?")

Obviously, some piece of those practices will entail the production of something like meaning for individuals or groups, but either way, at the end of the day, such musical meaning remains wholly a function of musical usage. For example, Bruce Springsteen's work may mean a lot to some people and not so much to others, but in whichever case, the music's meaning has everything to do with the contexts in which a person or group receives and uses it. The meaning of "Born to Run" isn't "in" the song but in the way that song functions for a particular individual or group—the emotions it provokes and the people or events that you associate with it. Which is at least partially to insist that any given practice's sociopolitical function (much less its meaning) can't really be decided from before the fact, and today's resistant, "authentic" practices certainly can't be guaranteed to function against the grain in an uncertain future. As we've seen, the hippie self-actualization ethos of the Grateful Dead certainly was seen as resistant to the disciplinary society of the mid-1960s, but today both the idea and the practices of hippiedom (be yourself, do your own thing) offer very little friction to dominant sociopolitical mandates of the twenty-first century. Be yourself and do your own thing is the mantra now routinely rehearsed everywhere from corporate wellness retreats to the pep talks offered by aging former sports stars at motivational seminars and Sunday morning prayer breakfasts.

At some level, this is more of what I call Foucault 101—"there are no machines of freedom, by definition," Foucault insists.[1] Actual freedom or resistance is not merely an idea, but it is only recognizable (or not) as the effect of a practice at a particular historical time and place. Likewise, it's never the subtending ground or original intention that guarantees the effect of a practice: for example, the insistence that any given music is "Not for Sale" may in fact function as that music's greatest sales slogan. Or we might note that dutifully following the injunction to "Rock and roll all night / and party every day" will in fact function to get you fired from the very band offering said advice, as Ace Frehley found out when he was booted out of Kiss.[2]

Methodologically speaking, this suggests that any cultural practices you'd want to examine—here, listening to popular music—will have to be stripped down to a certain level of commonality, or maybe even banality, before the respective functions of those practices can be investigated, examined, and discussed: the effects or the meaning of the song or musical form can't be guaranteed before the fact. And this means giving up, from the beginning, any sense that the function of the cultural artifact is dictated by the nature of the thing—for example, knowing from before the fact that X or Y artist is inauthentic pop or, conversely, that it's cutting edge, authentic, or whatever. As Frith phrases this methodological issue surrounding authentic versus inauthentic (worthy versus unworthy) music, "The problem with this argument is that . . . it is circular: an aesthetic judgement that [certain] songs are more 'authentic' than pop songs is the basis for the contrast between means of production (community creation v. commercial exploitation) which is used to explain why [these] songs are more authentic than pop songs."[3] In short, the logic of musical authenticity is completely tautological: it's merely the meshing of a set of premises ("West Coast rap rules!") with an example that fits those premises ("Tupac forever!"). As Nietzsche derisively comments on similar kinds of claims, it's like hiding something behind a bush, then finding it there later:[4] if you get to set up the premises for what counts as (in)authentic music, it shouldn't surprise you when you examine your chosen artist and come away with the desired results—depending on your criteria, either Lana Del Rey is or isn't worthy of critical attention.

Even in the best writing on popular music and its relations to neoliberal economics, one thing that remains nearly constant is the discursive move whereby the critic locates a privileged artist or group that somehow rises above the fray of commodified musical cooptation. Here, one thinks most infamously of Simon Frith's 1988 touting of the Pet Shop Boys as sharp purveyors of anticapitalist critique, a stance that seems more than a little bit puzzling today.[5] However, even in recent, very fine books on neoliberalism and music, there persists this critical drive to locate the resistant unicorn among the otherwise wholly commodified sounds of popular music. For example, in her *Resilience and Melancholy: Pop Music, Feminism, Neoliberalism*, Robin James locates Atari Teenage Riot's album *1995* as a linchpin instantiation of musical resistance to biopolitical capitalism, while Lady Gaga and Beyoncé function as the primary examples of capitulation to said capitalism and its insistence on a life of "resilience."[6] Likewise, Shank's *The Political Force of Musical Beauty* analyzes the Tuareg world-music group Tinariwen and the Velvet Underground's "Heroin," among others, as exemplary of the political force of popular music. While all of these analyses remain compelling on their own terms, less obvious to me is the critical apparatus whereby the Pet Shop Boys or Atari Teenage Riot or the Velvet Underground will somehow rise decisively above the Smiths or Borbetomagus or the Stooges (or for that matter, Frankie Goes to Hollywood, Kenny G, or 'N Sync) as privileged purveyors of a resistant musical *je ne sais quoi*. It all begins to look less like a critical analysis or diagnosis of a field and more like a savvy (neoliberal?) consumer's location and endorsement of the high-quality merchandise within that field.

In the end, if you want anything other than a kind of special pleading that confirms your own aesthetic likes and dislikes, you have to reduce the field to the banality of listening before you could begin to describe how and why listening to Canadian singer Justin Bieber is different from listening to Canadian singer Leonard Cohen. First, there's listening as a set of embedded social practices; then there's what that listening "means" (which is, of course, a subset of how that listening functions in a particular time and place). In short, to say "Leonard Cohen is better than Justin Bieber" ultimately begs the question, "Better for what?" For example, the only Bieber song I've ever heard in its entirety was played during an indoor cycling class at the gym—and it worked fine for that context (I wouldn't even have known it was Bieber's had the class instructor not apologized for the track beforehand). And as much as I admire Leonard Cohen's work, I can't imagine "Suzanne" or "Bird on a Wire" being "better" than almost any Bieber track when it comes to racing on an indoor bike.

As a field, cultural studies of popular music has—as Grossberg signals in his provocative critique—been oddly unwilling or unable to move beyond the terms of the debate set up in the 1930s, with authentic or challenging music posited as good and easily consumable music as bad. The "good" and "bad" (authentic and inauthentic) criteria can change over time or even invert (one can easily celebrate Elvis Presley as authentically "good" because of his popularity and wide-ranging cultural influences, while progressive rock like King Crimson is "bad" because it's so deliberately pompous and obscure). But the terms of the debate don't really change all that much, only the premises do. As I noted earlier, even the discourse of "poptimism"—giving up the "rockism" of individual (dis)taste and replacing it with the slogan "it's all good"—works on this same terrain, looking to elevate certain previously taboo musics to the point where they're considered worthy of critical consideration. The most successful book in this vein is probably Carl Wilson's *Let's Talk About Love: A Journey to the End of Taste*, his take on why we should treat Celine Dion's music (and her fan base) seriously. As I pointed out at the outset of this book, this poptimist move, however interesting or illuminating, doesn't challenge but in fact bolsters the Adorno-style logic of artistic worthiness by elevating a formerly neglected body of work into the lofty realm of commentary-worthy artifacts. Fans who already like Celine Dion—or other critical punching bags like Lil Wayne, Toby Keith, or Insane Clown Posse—could care less whether music critics take them seriously or not. It's only fellow music theorists who are likely to admire (or on the other side of the coin to be scandalized by) extended critical attention being paid to formerly lowbrow genres and artists.

Again, we see that the *logic* Adorno laid down for us (art versus commodity, high and low, worthy of commentary or not) remains largely untouched by the discourse of poptimism. It's just that in a biopolitical world, virtually everything becomes worthy of commentary and appreciation precisely because the measure of value is solely within the individual rather than value resting in the disciplinary logic of institutional mediation (and its avatars, the musical expert or the critic). If you like those songs or I like these artists, that's more than enough to make them worth listening to and talking about. As Tom Vanderbilt writes, poptimism really amounts to "taking the old highbrow strategy—the ability, wrote Bourdieu, to confidently 'constitute aesthetically objects that are ordinary or even common'—and bringing it to heretofore excluded musical genres."[7] Whatever magnanimous inclusiveness might accrue to the critical gesture of poptimism remains recognizable only to people who share the disdain formerly heaped on the likes of Celine Dion, while the gesture means little to nothing to those who have been her fans all along. After all, you have to be a highbrow critic to find lowbrow slumming laudable or theoretically interesting. As Bourdieu acidly puts it, "Populism is never anything other than an inverted ethnocentrism."[8]

And thereby the "critical" function of listening to music shifts from a disciplinary cordoning-off of tastes (certain institutionally sanctioned aesthetic premises dictate my listening choices and thereby brand me as the kind of subject dedicated to recognizable aesthetic discriminations) to a kind of free-for-all of individual eclecticism (me and my playlists, you and your playlists). When technology meets biopower and music becomes essentially ubiquitous (with the right equipment and connectivity, you can download or stream almost all the MP3s you want), music's taste-making function for any given individual shifts from one of narrow, disciplinary fealty to a world where the listener is less a critic than a kind of curator, putting interesting objects together to make a playlist. And here we see the shift from discipline to biopower yet again—the shifting function of music as a centrally important site of disciplinary training and identity (what you like or are willing to purchase in music situates you in a social space) to something distributed along the surface of your everyday life. Once the music is essentially ubiquitous, taste (which for Bourdieu implies scarcity and rigid hierarchy) gives way to curation in a world where almost everybody likes most genres and the music functions as a personal soundtrack for living (for example, high-energy dance music for the gym, low-energy emo for after midnight), as opposed to its disciplinary function within a series of public positionings—"Fuck you, I'm a punk rocker."

In tracing this discipline to biopower movement around the questions of eclecticism, consider for example the odd inversion that happens in Dan Fox's 2016 surprise bestseller *Pretentiousness: Why It Matters*. I had somehow thought, going into reading Fox's book, that the defense of pretentiousness would be an against-the-day resuscitation of the older, disciplinary sense of taste—insofar as the adjective "pretentious" tends to conjure someone like Adorno (or maybe SpongeBob's Squidward), who's almost slavishly dedicated to one (presumably high-culture) idea of worthiness, to the exclusion of all else. But it turns out that's not what Fox is interested in defending at all. Rather, pretentiousness for Fox functions as the opposite of that "my way or the highway" ethos you might associate with such titans of pretension as classical music snobs, continental philosophers, or lovers of conceptual art. In fact, it turns out that being pretentious in Fox's world is not at all associated with being a high-minded, exclusivist aesthete but instead involves intensifying a kind of biopolitical poptimist attitude—becoming a brave rule-breaker and experimenter, someone who's *not* dedicated to one mode of artistic value but rather open to appreciating everything.

As Fox writes, in a passage I can't be the only one to find completely counterintuitive, "Pretension is about over-reaching what you're capable of, taking the risk you might fall flat on your face. Without people stretching themselves and—self-consciously or otherwise—risking failure, most of the major works . . . that we cherish simply would not exist."[9] So pretentiousness, then, is not a snobby, singular commitment to some core set of principles but a concept that functions somewhat like the inspirational business slogans you could find festooning the employee lunch room at the insurance company (Give 110 Percent, Innovate, Don't Think with the Herd, Climb Your Own Personal Everest). Rather than hanging on to some stubborn aesthetic sense of what your tastes *really* are (a discourse that Fox derides as "authenticity"-talk), poptimist "pretentiousness" encourages you to remain open-minded, to consume it all—from Taylor Swift to Cat Power, from lunch at McDonald's to dinner at the Korean BBQ.

In fact, these biopolitical days, the dedicated "rockist" is now in danger of being labeled as an inauthentic, knuckle-dragging "univore"—as Vanderbilt defines them, "people who listen to the fewest genres and express the most disliking for other music genres"—rather than a poptimistic omnivore, who happily consumes all kinds of music.[10] In stark contrast to the way you could have easily diagnosed a highbrow in the 1950s by his single-minded, snobbish love of European classical music (I'm looking at you, Teddy Adorno), Vanderbilt reminds us that today such cultural "univores tend to be lower-educated people in groups with lesser cultural status."[11] Midcentury discipline trained your musical tastes and linked that training to a series of class-inflected cultural sites: you could tell something concrete about people if they talked about music primarily in terms of the school, the church, the Cotton Club, Studio 54, MTV, the Mudd Club, the rave, the local record store, the opera house, or the Beatles at Shea Stadium. On the other hand, biopower radically deterritorializes these questions of taste (everything from "likes" on Facebook to Yelp reviews to thumbs up or down on a Spotify stream) and thereby delinks taste from traditional sites of competition for cultural capital. In a biopolitical world taste finds itself largely governed not by an institutional hierarchy but by subjects saddled with the burden of constantly constructing their own personal identity.

In other words, despite all demographic evidence to the contrary, there remains a strong ideological thread within biopower suggesting it really *does* matter whether I like Beyoncé or not. And of course, in some senses that's true: despite the ways the world has changed since Bourdieu did his fieldwork on taste and social categorization, if you say, for example, in an academic setting that you *don't* like Beyoncé (or worse that you don't like sushi or that you voted for Trump), eyebrows will be raised—less so, one assumes, than if you profess you don't like Beyoncé at a NASCAR race. Of course, in actuality it doesn't really make any demographic difference whether any one person likes Beyoncé or votes Republican (pop music hits and elections are mass phenomena wherein any single individual's choices are irrelevant). But these choices do continue to function in the local, everyday arena of personal identity production and management, and these preferences also function decisively as raw, entry-level information to be collated and sold as big data informatics. Again and again we see the drama of biopower played out: individual lives, tastes, and identities immediately cross-referenced not so much with institutional power hierarchies but with mass demographic patterns of likes and dislikes.

Hence popular music's continued importance as that "inside/outside" bridge that biopower needs for its operating system to function—as a way to link up broad-based demographic trends with seemingly very personal investments. Millions of people worldwide love Kendrick Lamar, but not in the way I do personally. Vanderbilt highlights this mass-authenticity biopolitical drama when he narrates his initial interview with the music-streaming service Pandora, which does not desire to discipline, dictate, or hierarchize tastes but to track them in a biopolitical way: "They wanted me to know," Vanderbilt writes, "they were not 'tastemakers in any sense of the word.' Rather, they strove to 'provide each and every listener with a unique experience,'"[12] to connect intense personal investments with a broad demographic style or sound of music, thereby creating not a mass identity to which one must conform (sooooo disciplinary, that) but biopower's signature "unique experience" for "each and every listener."

As Pandora hit the fifty billion (!) mark for collected rat-ings (thumbs up or down) in early 2015, we clearly see personal taste—I like this, I don't like this—meeting big data (as fifty billion song ratings works out to an average of more than seven songs rated by every person on the planet, though as of 2017 Spotify has almost twice as many subscribers as Pandora, thereby possessing even bigger data to mine). And with "likes" comes a taste profile, constructed by mass algorithmic data disaggre-gation. As Pandora's chief algorithm writer reports, "There's no accounting for [individual] taste. But we can account for it, en masse. We can say there's an 84 percent chance that this song is going to work for people listening to the Rolling Stones radio. It's a good bet; we've accounted for the taste of this big group of people."[13]

8

In the Mood

Bourdieu's work clearly shows us that personal taste preferences—or what he dubs "distinction strategies"—have performed their disciplinary work of class stratification through the biopolitical social work of slotting any particular user into a mass demographic pattern. For Bourdieu, however, a disciplinary notion of class remains the dominant overarching grid of intelligibility that makes social sense of individual tastes. As Adorno famously phrases a similar sentiment in *Dialectic of Enlightenment*, in a consumer society, "Something is provided for everyone so that no one can escape."[1] Indeed, across class lines in the late disciplinary society of the twentieth century, there remained a robust emergent biopolitical market for some kind of *escape* from the boredom and uniformity of everyday capitalist life. And one can trace that desire for finding escape in popular music from the jitterbugging and swing dancing of the Depression, through the desire for escape written into the lyrics of the rock, punk, and hip-hop eras (sentiments well summed up in Grossberg's song-lyric book title, *We Gotta Get Out of This Place*), all the way to today's celebratory poptimism, which seeks escape from the rockist sense of exclusive musical commitments.

Take, as an intense contemporary example of that desire for escape, the booming business of streaming music over the internet—offered up by contemporary giants like Spotify, Google Play, iTunes, and Pandora. These music-providing services don't so much sell music—MP3 downloads or dusty vinyl through the mail—as they sell biopolitical consciousness enhancement or mood and attention (dis)connectivity. You require certain streams of music for various means of escape: escape from boredom while plowing through quarterly reports at work (music for focus and attention); escape while driving home after work (depending on the day and/or the traffic, maybe a mellowing chill-out mix or an angry fist-pumping one); a very different kind of stream for escaping fatigue during your gym workout (high BPM or anthemic music); or a "Gin and Juice" stream for escaping the world of work and toil altogether in setting up the soundtrack for your party Saturday night. As Paul Allen Anderson puts it, "Whether at work, home, the mall, the gym, on the bus or in the car, web-connected subjects live and weave among an array of streaming platforms for algorithmic or curated musical moodscapes and affective atmospheres."[2]

In the disciplinary era pervasive mood-altering music went by the brand name Muzak, which was in turn the epitome of musical Fordism's understanding of escape (one smooth, seamless style of elevator music for escaping or assuaging the tedium of disciplinary institutions piped into the workplace, the shopping mall, the waiting room, or even on Muzak LPs for the home). By contrast the biopolitical force of internet streaming is all about niche markets, about harnessing and augmenting the individual authenticity effects associated with popular music. Just as the most obvious example, you may have noticed that there's no elevator music played in elevators anymore. My students in fact barely recognize Muzak or only recall it through shadow memories: the soundtrack for waiting in line with Mom at the

JCPenney in central Arkansas, as one grad student recently put it. In the Fordist institutions of the not-so-distant past, only the blandest of soundtracks were available as you shopped, sat at your desk, or cleaned up the break room. Muzak was specifically designed to ward off the soul-stealing compulsions of discipline, to keep you on task as you shopped or worked. In a disciplinary world, wherein as Foucault reminds us power *acts on actions*, Muzak kept you focused on what you were doing and concomitantly kept at bay any kind of biopolitical self-reflexivity—for example you thinking to yourself, "This job sucks."

However, in a biopolitical world, listening to "your music"—and harnessing the positive mood-effects, the momentary reflexivity or escape that it evokes—can make popular music an affective ally to be courted by employers and ad agencies rather than a distraction-inducing demon to be left in the car's eight-track tape player when you arrive at the job or the mall. As Anderson writes, "listening to individually preferred music (in other words, music to which a given listener attaches a personal history of emotionally pleasant memories) fuels productivity and employee satisfaction in a digitally-oriented workplace,"[3] which leads to a contemporary biopolitical landscape where popular music quite literally sets the tone or mood: "more than ever before, individuals' ostensibly private lives with music and especially with the moods and emotions stirred by pre-ferred recordings have become assets for affective labor in the workplace."[4] In the shift from disciplinary power to biopower, popular music—especially rock and rap—has gone from being excluded in the workplace (as a dangerous distraction and potential morale problem) to constituting a welcome means for attention focus and positive mood alteration. How else could the house band play David Bowie's "Station to Station" during a break at the hyper-conservative 2016 Republican Convention?

("It's not the side effects of the cocaine / I'm thinking that it must be Trump.")

In fact, Jonathan Beller argues that attracting and managing human attention has become *the* hot commodity of the twenty-first century, and a quick Google search will concur—as one website puts it straightforwardly, "Attention is now the ultimate commodity." In her article "I Attend, Therefore I Am," philosopher and cognitive scientist Carolyn Dicey Jennings goes so far as to redefine human subjectivity not in terms of our reasoning or language-using abilities but in terms of our capability to pay attention: "the self comes into being with the first act of attention, or the first time attention favours one interest over another."[5] (One is tempted here to insert a comment about the Lacanian mirror stage relocated to the clothing-store fitting room, but I will defer.) Behind this turn to attention economics is a larger biopolitical harnessing of the productivities of everyday human life, including the body and the senses, within an expanding world-media system. Just to take the most obvious example, in a disciplinary society the workday was pretty much over when you clocked out or left the office. Not anymore, as smartphones, email, texts, FaceTime, Skype, and a hundred other web- and app-based intrusions make it clear you can never escape from your job—both your actual job (what you do for a living) and the ancillary job you have as a productive consumer who's in charge of endlessly remolding your life.

With a relatively inexpensive smartphone and a Wi-Fi or data connection, you can pay attention—that is to say, you can buy things, answer email, read reviews, track a delivery, hail a ride, or update Facebook—from virtually anywhere, at any time. As Beller puts it in his article "Paying Attention,"

> we have entered into a period characterized by the full incorporation of the sensual by the economic. This incorporation

of the senses along with the dismantling of the word emerges through the visual pathway as new orders of machine-body interface. . . . All evidence points in this direction: that in the twentieth century, capital first posited and now presupposes looking as productive labor, and, more generally, posited attention as productive of value.[6]

Beller's argument revolves around cinema as an intense site of training in the early twentieth century. In his view the movie theater constituted a kind of factory for training spectators to extract value from their attention, a testing ground for the biopolitical expansion of capitalism into everyday life. In *The Cinematic Mode of Production: Attention Economy and the Society of the Spectacle*, Beller goes so far as to call this new form the "attention theory of value": "What I will call 'the attention theory of value' finds in the notion of 'labor', elaborated in Marx's labor theory of value, the prototype of the newest source of value production under capitalism today: value-producing human attention."[7] And this attention theory of value constitutes an experimental R&D operation within each of us, a biopolitical niche market of one wherein "new affects, aspirations, and forms of interiority are experiments in capitalist productivity."[8]

In the one hundred years since the disciplinary era of the cinema's emergence (Beller talks largely about early modernist film, Vertov and Eisenstein), we've seen a decisive intensification and general spread of such attention labor into your home through television and into your everyday routines through the near-ubiquity of computer and smartphone screens today, where it seems everyone's always looking at something. In short, modes of focusing our distributed attention are the hot advertising and business commodities of our time. As Beller reminds us, "perception is increasingly bound to [value] production"[9]—think of the way the stock market fluctuates with changing perceptions about the future, or the ways that brands are managed not by making changes in the products but largely through influencing consumers' feelings about them. And most obviously, various forms of click-bait on the internet are vying for attention as value: you have to click through for someone to get paid, and before you can click through, something first has to draw your attention.

Beller convincingly shows us how the movie theater was a visual factory for mass training in disciplinary capitalism, and watching remains an important pedagogical practice for the intensification of subjective attention in the move from discipline to biopower (from the theater to the home TV and finally to the portable ubiquity of the smartphone screen). However, I'd like to suggest along a parallel track that the *soundtrack* of the attention economy has become even more crucial as a transversal operating system for biopower. Attali famously argues that sound is more important than vision to the human sensorium: "The world is not for beholding. It is for hearing. It is not legible, but 'audible.'"[10] While I don't know whether we need to decide finally or definitively whether sound is more important than vision in harvesting value from subjects in the era of biocapitalism, I argue that the saturated ubiquity of music over the past several decades has brought it tightly into the everyday sensorium in a way even more intense than the saturation of visual images within our lives. In short, I'm arguing here that listening practices enjoy a privilege over visual practices as the canary in the coal mine that is the attention theory of value. Ironically, music usurps this privileged place as a linchpin for examining the workings of biopolitical capitalism precisely because of popular music's more or less unconscious mode of working on subjects (because music works directly on mood, affect, and memory).

Take, for example, this incident that happened to me recently. I was driving west into the low, intense, setting sun late one afternoon, not-listening to the radio (which sucks in central Pennsylvania), when I found myself humming a Warren Zevon song, "Desperados under the Eaves," with its great lines "Don't the sun look angry through the trees," in the end only confirming that the sun is finally "angry at me."[11] It was one of those little moments where we like to think popular music enriches our lives through a momentary escape from the mundane—making connections, perfectly summing up an experience, indeed prolonging it and connecting it to prior moments scattered across the welter of experiences that make up your life, perhaps offering a moment of epiphany, or maybe just respite from the dullness of the task at hand, driving to pick up the kids. "I haven't heard that song in years," I thought to myself, so when I got home, I walked right past my CD collection (now in neglected shambles, though Zevon would have been easy enough to find, as it's somewhere near the end of the alphabetical line, right after Zappa) and directly pulled the song up on YouTube. Ahh, yes, there it is—a lot more orchestrated than I'd remembered it (were those introductory strings always there?), but still great stuff.

Listening to it for a second time, I glance down at the comment lines under the YouTube clip. The first says, "Ray Donovan sent me here." What? Several of the next comments also mention *Ray Donovan*, the SHOWTIME series (which I watch regularly) starring Liev Schreiber and Jon Voight. So I think to myself, ahh, the show always closes with a song to sum up the episode. The producers must have used the Zevon song at some point during the show's run, and the comments are left over from whenever that episode aired. I feel like it's nice that the show helps people discover new music (or at least music that's new to them—the Zevon song's from the mid-1970s), but I wonder whether it's also embarrassingly lame to have your musical tastes curated for you by a visual mass medium like television. And I likewise wonder what kind of internet cred you can garner by boasting about how you'd never heard the song before it showed up on a TV show. (It's hard to imagine someone in my youth bragging, "Man, I heard a great song playing over the credits of last week's *Starsky & Hutch* episode.") Yet another post tries to one-up the *Ray Donovan* crowd: this person claims to have been into Zevon much longer, since way back in 2013, when his music was featured on *Californication*, another popular cable-TV series. The Adorno in me immediately pictures this as Pavlovian spoon-feeding of the uninformed musical masses (desper-dildos, I ventured), who again and again find themselves falling for a cross-platform marketing strategy masquerading as personal and musical discovery.

I look at the dates of the comments to see exactly when the episode aired because I didn't remember the song being used in the show. It's only then I see that the *Ray Donovan* comments are from today and yesterday. Meaning the show aired only a few days ago . . . and I in fact saw it. Now I remember, and it all comes back to me: the whole reason I found myself humming the song today was because I'd heard it a few days ago playing under the credits of a visual medium, a TV show. But I'd of course forgotten that, and the song seeped in under the conscious radar of the visual image to lodge itself as an earworm that would slither back up to the conscious level when the sun-drenched scenery was right, when my visual field (intense sunlight) needed a soundtrack.[12] The song is still playing on YouTube, and this all occurs to me right at the point where the song pivots to the chorus, and Zevon laughs to mark the transition, "Ha, don't the sun look angry." "Ha," Zevon seems sardonically to taunt me, "you're here for the same reason as that sea of lame-os, because you heard a song on a TV show, and you wanted to hear it again. At least they admit why they're here, because they're slaves to the culture industry. What's your excuse?" Far from the savvy critic autonomously recalling the perfect song to supplement the moment, I find myself instead to be someone stupid enough to think that the song came to me, and I came to YouTube, of my own free will, experiencing a spontaneous moment of inspiration with this Warren Zevon song after not having heard it for probably twenty years. Sure, right. Who's the desper-dildo now?

In short, precisely because biopolitical lifestyle capitalism feeds on the links between deeply personal (sometimes even unconscious) tastes and mass demographic patterns, popular music is *the* privileged site for examining the workings of biopower, a power that works across the surface and in the viscera of your everyday life. And one of the primary uses or functions of popular music (which is less a thing than a set of listening practices made almost seamlessly ubiquitous by the MP3, internet streaming, and the smartphone) has everything to do with music's being stretched across the other senses and their links to attention and memory: evoking a past state of satisfaction or well-being, focusing attention on particular tasks, setting the stage or creating the mood everywhere from the mall and the Starbucks to home soundscaping like the Luther Vandross date night mix or Dean Martin for cocktail hour. Of course, ubiquitous music can also disengage attention from the tasks at hand, especially in its shoe-gazing, chill-out, or ambient forms, and thereby music can perform a kind of utopian (if momentary) disentanglement from the attention economy of biopower (more on this below). But as Vanderbilt sums up its biopolitical privilege, "Music is what people do on their own: in the car, with their headphones, via their playlists and customized stations. Preferences for it are strongly personal, and people will talk about 'my music' in a way they do not talk about 'my movies.'"[13]

9

Will There Be Music?

In a very famous passage Adorno wonders out loud: after the unthinkably horrific production of corpses in the factories that were the Third Reich's death camps, could there be anything lofty like poetry after Auschwitz? Or did high art and its autonomous aesthetic realm get burned up in those concentration camps as well?[1] This remains a haunting question. But precious few thinkers, as Beller reminds us, wondered if there could be movies after such barbarity, and even fewer I'd venture wondered if there could be popular music after the horrors of World War II, because popular culture exists, at least in part, to produce some kind of integration—to produce belief in a world without anything much to believe in. Beller writes, "As global trends from statistical marketing to new social movements to the new fundamentalisms imply in as much as they represent the *formation* of nontraditional forms of social agency and action, belief is bought and sold, it organizes, it produces, it is, in short, labor. The labor of belief is one of the strong forms of what I call the *productive value of human attention.*"[2]

Thereby popular culture, as Adorno shows us in his "Culture Industry" essay, becomes a mode of production in its own right—finding its end-product not in songs or films or TV shows but in the form of subjects, prosumers who produce their whole lives out of their consumption patterns. As I've said from the outset, though, I'm not so much interested in further developing the Adornian line of argumentation that Beller extends so artfully—showing how film brings about the reign of commodity spectatorship through an "industrialization of the sensorium."[3] I'm interested not so much in critiquing the disciplinary industrial training of our senses (Adorno does that work spectacularly) but rather in the biopoliticization of the sensorium that comes through sound, particularly through popular music. What I'm arguing here is that, for better or worse, today popular music functions more as a biopolitical mood enhancement technology than it does as a disciplinary training mechanism: music is less a matter of consciousness being trained to make sense of images (the visual culture thesis that Beller offers) than it is a matter of moods being managed aurally. Beller convincingly makes his argument about attention and value in terms of cinema and its disciplining of vision, but here I'm trying to extend and intensify these questions of value and the sensorium into the realm of popular music (and its somewhat different biopolitical role in governing individuals).

But just in passing I'd note that one could construct a similar argument concerning attention, value, and the senses not only for film or TV but in terms of Euro-American museum art in the twentieth century. Virtually everything having to do with "artfulness," from Dada forward, shifts art's value from the object (and from the question of representation) to the kind of attention paid to the object once it's brought into a museum or gallery space: from Hugo Ball's performances and Duchamp's urinal through Jackson Pollock's splatter works, Jean-Michel Basquiat's layered semiotic universe, and Cindy Sherman's movie stills, all the way to conceptual art, whose anticommodity stance (so much like popular music's) barely conceals the ways in which the high art scene over the past few decades has constituted an immense economics seminar in Beller's "attention theory of value." Which is to say, we learn from contemporary art the invaluable lesson that drawing attention to an object or practice, then manipulating or even merely holding that attention, has become the most highly prized marker of cultural "value" in our time.

This turn to the biopolitical subject as producer of artistic value also reveals for us the mistake continually made by the exasperated parents in the museum, looking at a Duchamp hat-rack, a Paul Klee painting, or a Jenny Holzer scroll of banal phrases on a pixel screen, shaking their head and saying, "My kid could do that." For the expert, of course, this kind of comment immediately rebounds onto the person making the judgment, who seems not to realize that the artfulness isn't in the object, but in the kind of attention that the object asks you to pay to it: the way the artwork invites *you* to infuse the work with artfulness and thereby separate it from the common mass of artless things. This move to elevate the everyday is of course the holy grail of the attention economy, and we can see how the high-art markets of the twentieth century were the attention-grabbing proving grounds for the clickbait advertising and endless Facebook posting of today, desperate to draw a certain kind of attention in order to add value to an otherwise worthless practice or object.

Bourdieu points out that modern art requires much from its consumers, as it is the beholder's attention (not the objects themselves) that must finally articulate the "artistic" quality of otherwise mundane objects in a gallery:

> Never perhaps has more been asked of the spectator, who is now required to "re-produce" the primary operation whereby the artist (with the complicity of his whole intellectual field) produced this new fetish. But never perhaps has he been given so much in return. The naive exhibitionism of "conspicuous consumption," which seeks distinction in the crude display

of ill-mastered luxury, is nothing compared to the unique capacity of the pure gaze, a quasi-creative power which sets the aesthete apart from the common herd by a radical difference which seems to be inscribed in "persons." . . . The new art is not for everyone, like Romantic art, but destined for an especially gifted minority.[4]

What Bourdieu describes in the 1960s as a class-mobile striving (to accumulate cultural capital, to allow the artist or art lover to break out of the class strictures inherent in Bourdieu's midcentury, Fordist, disciplinary society) has intensified and spread to become the central pillar of the logic of everyday identity in the biopolitical era—where no one is comfortable being ordinary, and everyone is charged with the task of infusing his or her life with meaningfulness, making your life a work of art.

And in a manner similar to the functioning of high-art tastes in the disciplinary era, popular musical tastes in the biopolitical era allow one to accumulate cultural capital, to be recognized as a certain kind of savvy MP3 curator: like knowing a lot about museum art in previous eras, having something to say about popular music today "helps the 'best' to know and recognize one another in the greyness of the multitude and to learn their mission, which is to be few in number and to have to fight against [disappearing into] the multitude."[5] Just mention the Canadian power trio Rush to a white guy over the age of fifty, or mention Drake to anyone under thirty, and you can see what Bourdieu means. However, this mission of personal branding, of not disappearing into the crowd, is no longer merely the purview of the upper classes and the striving artist class, as it is in Bourdieu's disciplinary analysis. This manufacturing and updating of identity, this constant remaking of your life, is the everyday job of each and every one of us in a biopolitical world.

10

Bourdieu, Bourdon't

When he talks about taste as a marker of class power and mobility, many commentators take Bourdieu to be arguing for a notion of class performance, maybe something akin to Fox's "pretentiousness": a kind of social pretending or performativity designed and calculated to provoke, to invent, or otherwise to help the subject get ahead by substituting largely fictitious *cultural* capital for real *economic* capital. Such a reading of Bourdieu, however, intensifies an argumentative mistake that I think haunted the discourse surrounding Judith Butler's gender performativity for many years: to wit, just because you argue that some deeply held interior state is socially constructed (aesthetic taste for Bourdieu or gender identity for Butler), it doesn't necessarily follow that the belief is based on a rational, self-interested calculation or voluntaristic choice among alternatives. This is how many people (mis)understood Butler's work on gender performativity for years—taking it to be saying something like "in order to gain some kind of cultural or personal advantage in the social field, I want to act like a man today," which could perhaps be translated into Bourdieu's tastemaking idiom as "in order to gain some traction with lovers of *Portlandia*, I want to profess that I like Sleater-Kinney today."

However, as both Bourdieu and Butler have argued in their own ways, the social construction of identity does not necessarily imply a subjective decisionism: you can have a deeply held, indeed nearly unshakeable, sense of your gender identity or your aesthetic tastes, but it doesn't necessarily follow from there that sexual or artistic preference is either a "natural" phenomenon or a merely conveniently chosen one, precisely because social systems canalize and naturalize behavior just as efficiently as—if not more so than—neurochemical and genetic phenomena. As Bourdieu writes, "Each taste feels itself to be natural—and so it almost is, being a habitus."[1] Of course, unlike investments in gender identity, few would argue that deeply held aesthetic tastes are natural in the scientific sense (there's no gene to explain why people like Katy Perry), but Bourdieu is keen to point out that they're not *simply* calculating choices either because we are all products of a sociopolitical system of practices—a constraining field and habitus—that we can't fully account for. We constantly make investments in a cultural taste market, making moves in a series of cultural games, but we hardly control the rules of those games.

While Bourdieu's work is saturated with economic metaphors (class distinction, cultural capital, artistic markets), he is quick to clarify that although the "terms are borrowed from the language of economics, it is in no way suggested that the corresponding behavior is guided by rational calculation of maximum profit, as the ordinary usage of these concepts, no doubt mistakenly, implies."[2] "Rational calculation" doesn't control these taste-discrimination processes, but not because these investments are simply irrational. Rather, these cultural economies and individual investments are guided by a habitus that makes them seem inevitable, especially to the investors: "Culture is the site, par excellence, of misrecognition, because, in generating strategies objectively adapted to the objective chances of profit of which it is the product, the sense of investment secures profits which do not need to be pursued as profits" because of their "being seen (and seeing themselves) as perfectly disinterested, unblemished by any cynical or mercenary use of culture."[3] This seeming aesthetic disinterest is of course the primary difference in Bourdieu between markets of "real" capital and markets of "cultural" capital: those seeking cultural capital are in the end just as mercenary as seekers of craven cash profits, but cultural strivers are able to (mis)recognize what they're doing as a disinterested pursuit of aesthetic experience. If you're trading stocks, everyone assumes you're in it for the money; if you're trading opinions on old-school hip-hop or Bob Dylan's Nobel Prize, it has to seem like you're doing so for other than self-interested reasons. As Bourdieu puts it, "the structure of the distribution of economic capital is symmetrical and opposite to that of cultural capital,"[4] at least partially because to enhance your cultural capital, you have to seem like you're not trying or you don't care (posed, self-assured bohemianism). And you certainly can't get there as a biopolitical striver by nakedly lusting after cultural capital (whereas craven cash-lust doesn't really make any difference if you're looking to line your pockets with economic capital).

   This distinction between economic and cultural capital is what Fran Lebowitz exploits when she quips that Donald Trump represents "a poor person's idea of a rich person."[5] Which is to say that, in general, savvy rich people aren't at all like Trump because they assiduously avoid exhibiting the cultural stereotypes surrounding money-grubbing businessmen: thin-skinned, obviously both greedy and needy, always calling attention to their wealth (a real no-no if you actually are wealthy), and willing to plaster gilt over all the tacky conspicuous consumption objects they surround themselves with. But that's what poor people understand rich people to be, and Trump fits the suit perfectly. For Bourdieu, "the exchange rate of different kinds of capital is one of the fundamental stakes in the struggles between class fractions,"[6] and on his account, cultural aesthetes who pretend to eschew market striving (people like Fran Lebowitz) are highly efficient self-deceivers—in eager pursuit of higher returns on a different stock exchange, the cultural capital market. And Lebowitz's comments concerning Trump supporters are nothing if not highly condescending toward people with low levels of cultural capital: "They see him. They think, 'If I were rich, I'd have a fabulous tie like that. Why are my ties not made of 400 acres of polyester?' All that stuff he shows you in his house—the gold faucets—if you won the lottery, that's what you'd buy."[7] Taste, as Bourdieu insists, is simply class warfare by other means.

As an aside, one might here begin to wonder: has the logic of economic capital in the biopolitical era simply collapsed into the logic of Bourdieu's cultural capital and vice versa? We live in a world where even minimum-wage workers have to innovate and be mindful, while at the high end of finance, insurance, and real estate, financial value depends less on assets backed by "real" economic capital than they do on market perception. Indeed, couldn't Trump's career be read as one long Bourdieu seminar in "distinction," branding everything from steaks and wine to Trump University and the White House with his signature mass-appeal bravado? In any case, we live in a biopolitical world where taste canalizes preferences and allows any given striving subject to jockey for constantly floating portfolios of cultural capital. But of course, you, whoever you might be, don't get to construct the social field or make the rules of that taste game, so your agency is constrained to the moves that the game makes available.

But this is where a certain kind of rationalist voluntarism returns in Bourdieu through the back door, insofar as taste is a constant self-branding mechanism in Bourdieu's discourse, a constant economic hoarding of the scarce goods of cultural capital and recognition and is thereby precisely about making self-interested choices in a field where you're vying for a certain kind of control. For Bourdieu, taste is primarily a social game of jockeying for distinction—"a space of objective positions to which corresponds a homologous space of stances or position-takings (which operates as a space of possibilities or options given to participants in the field at any given moment)."[8] In short, the field itself opens various "objective positions" or options to social players at any given moment. And even if the game of taste is not exactly about sovereign choice (at the end of the day, you finally do have to order from the menu of available options), for Bourdieu taste is not about vulgar conspicuous consumption (acquiring the *objects* that keep up with the Joneses) but about what we might call a highly nuanced inconspicuous consumption (adopting positions that keep up with the *tastes* of the Joneses), and therefore the game of distinction is just as much a rationalist choosing mechanism as it is one of social compulsion. You still choose from constrained available objects and opinions, but the right choice leads you to be a winner in the game of cultural capital and/or to get more substantial return on your cultural investments. Given the way we size up our options and exercise our taste accordingly, we can further our personal economic interests if we make the correct decision.

In his own habitus, the heavily class-stratified Gaullist years in France (remember, all his field work on cultural tastes was done before the May 1968 upheavals), Bourdieu's work is undoubtedly illuminating. But I wonder how well (if at all) his work translates to questions about class and taste stratification in twenty-first-century North America. And I wonder about this less because I think economic stratification has somehow lessened over the past fifty years in America and elsewhere (quite the opposite, as any Google search will tell you), but because the "cultural capital" game of mobility is today less a strategy that only some people (with education, connections, style) can choose to play.

Rather, the brand-yourself roulette of social identity has become the game that all of us are compelled to play in the neoliberal, biopolitical world of the adolescent twenty-first century.

Lord knows, class hierarchy is alive and well in the United States, but the current situation is not really analogous to the situation of 1960s France. For example, the highly strati-fied class context of Bourdieu's day is shown in the musical objects he serves up for the aesthetic judgment of his control group. The "middlebrow" songs on offer to Bourdieu's survey participants—"Blue Danube" and "Hungarian Rhapsody"—would for today's American music consumer seem hopelessly highbrow, though today's American music consumer might know Queen's "Bohemian Rhapsody." In Bourdieu's schema, "*'popular' taste*" is represented by "works of so-called 'light' music or classical music devalued by popularization, such as the *Blue Danube*. . . , *La Traviata*, or *L'Arlésienne*, and especially songs totally devoid of artistic ambition or pretension such as those of Luis Mariano, Guétary or Petula Clark."[9] Perhaps the biggest difference between Bourdieu's moment in the early to midsixties and ours is that there is little to no popular music these days that is "totally devoid of artistic ambition or pre-tension" (even Justin Bieber talks about himself as an artist). Recall that it is only in the midsixties that popular music found itself making widespread "artistic" claims at all—people usually point to the Beatles' 1967 *Sgt. Pepper's Lonely Hearts Club Band* as the origin—but those claims are now both ubiquitous and necessary within the field of popular music, as everyone has become a kind of stakeholder in the game of popular music, as well as a stakeholder in the game of constantly updating and remaking your identity (a field or habitus that was largely confined to the educated classes in disciplinary Gaullist France). Indeed, cultural arenas that were for Bourdieu extraeduca-tionally lowbrow—he writes about cultural "areas, like cinema or jazz, which are neither taught nor directly assessed by the educational system"[10]—have in the ensuing years become fully incorporated into schools and universities, just as the game of musical taste has been fully exported from institutions and into the streets: the movement from discipline (with its critics and taste-making institutions) to biopower (with people constantly updating their performative identity productions in tune with the soundtrack of their lives).

In any case, I linger here on the relations between Butler's performativity and Bourdieu's habitus because despite obvious similarities among these two kinds of social compulsion—performative gender identity and aesthetic class identity—I see Butler's performativity functioning differently. This is precisely because it is an idea steeped in a culturally dominant biopower (the identity politics world of the 1990s, where everything moves through personal identity), while Bourdieu's work on aesthetic discrimination remains a remnant of the disciplinary world of class stratification, before the biopolitical gender and race identity revolutions of the late sixties. In short, identity for Bourdieu remains first and foremost class identity wherein whatever limited class mobility exists can in fact be calculated within a fairly rigid social hierarchy. Whereas for Butler class certainly remains a factor in terms of performativity, in her theory of gender identity, class could never have an absolute privilege among a series of other biopolitical, intersectional identity factors—race, gender, sexual orientation, ethnicity, age, (dis)ability, and so on.

For Bourdieu, economic class is determining in the last instance (as it structures the field and parses out the various positions one might assume within the habitus, rationally or otherwise), while for Butler, a long series of intersectional identity factors remains just as important as (if not more important than) economic factors in configuring the habitus of her era.

But that's still not exactly the point I want to make with the comparison of Bourdieu and Butler. The specific point, rather, is that as a theory, Butler's gender performativity is just as steeped in the economic conditions of its time as Bourdieu's; however, it's the economic conditions themselves that will have changed drastically between the early 1960s (when Bourdieu is doing his field work) and the early 1990s (the high-theory era of identity politics, the original historical terrain of Butler's work in the United States). In the thirty years of history that separate these theoretical paradigms, what changes is not so much any given theory's imbrication with the economic imperatives dominant in its moment of historical emergence; rather, what changes are those dominant economic imperatives themselves. In short, what counts as a properly economic question within the midcentury, disciplinary, essentially Fordist capitalism of Bourdieu's era will not be the same as what counts as an economic question within the biopolitical finance capitalism of our era. It's no longer possible, to put it bluntly, simply to pit "proper" economic questions of class (questions of the productive economic base) against fanciful questions of social identity (superstructural questions), precisely because social questions of identity fuel the economic imperatives of our biopolitical day.[11] What's changed from disciplinary to biopolitical capitalism, in other words, is the very intense becoming-economic of what used to be thought of as merely cultural questions about identity or personal tastes and desires. Within the attention economy of biopower, these "inside" questions about personal identity or desire have met up with "outside" questions of economic class and finance.[12] As Foucault puts it, in a biopolitical world "the class struggle still exists, it exists more intensely," distributed across the surfaces of our lives and identities, rather than being enforced from above or below everyday life by the various Ideological State Apparatuses that train and constrain us.[13]

11

Everywhere, All the Time

All along I've insisted that it's the "mass culture" quality of popular music that interests me; in addition, it's popular music's ubiquity (and maybe even its banality—the very reasons that someone like Adorno refused to take it seriously) that to my mind makes music the skeleton key to understanding changes in both cultural production and subject production over the second half of the twentieth century and into the twenty-first. Just like everybody else, I'm not like everybody else.

But what exactly do I mean by saying that popular music is more central than other cultural forms for understanding the recent American cultural past and the present? Well, certainly in my lifetime, it's become very hard indeed to make convincing and sweeping cultural claims for literature or museum art as mass drivers of anything in particular in terms of widespread cultural effects on contemporary subjectivity. Today, for better or worse, high art forms circulate in a niche market, like eBay collectibles, and as such are not really a mass pivot for diagnosing large-scale changes in contemporary subjectivity. But that doesn't stop art critics and literature scholars (people like me) from making all sorts of breathless mass cultural claims in the pages of academic journals—articles on "The Environmental Politics of Jorie Graham" or "Neoliberal Motifs in Jeff Koons."

Surely literature or museum art can perform cultural work, but if you're looking for a recent art form that's influential on a mass scale, you'd have to admit that most Americans don't read contemporary poetry or really have much to say about art retrospectives.

But millions of people in the United States still do have an iPod, and as of January 2017, around 90 percent of Americans age eighteen to forty-nine use a smartphone, most of them stocked with MP3s (organized into custom playlists).[1] Likewise, millions of people worldwide have Spotify, Pandora, or other internet streams going much of the day (at work, on the bus, and at home), as well as satellite radio in the car for the commute. There's also popular music playing prominently within myriad other cultural forms that we encounter every day—TV shows and advertisements, video games, films, not to mention the ubiquitous pop soundtrack playing at the mall, the gym, the fast-food place, the dentist's office, and the grocery store. Popular music presently enjoys a saturation level within everyday life that remains very much unlike any other contemporary art form. And as such, it's a particularly intense example of Guattari's "machinic enslavement" (or government of dividuals) within the biopolitical control society.

In terms of its functioning, popular music's ubiquity allows it to operate at a largely subconscious level of the refrain—as you realize every time you find yourself humming some song you heard somewhere. At least for me, it's pretty easy to tune out the Fox News feed playing on the doctor's waiting-room TV—often by throwing on the earbuds and listening to my own music. Or if you forgot your earbuds, you can just look away from the screen, because you have to pay a certain level of attention to be affected by visual media like television. However, it's much harder to tune out the soundtrack in the waiting room— precisely because you don't have to pay conscious attention to the music, but it continues to work on you nevertheless. Later in the day you find yourself humming the words or toe-tapping the riff from some Motown song.

I wish neither to decry this functioning of popular music as sinister mind control nor to find within it some hidden subversion (a debate whose terms constitute another of Grossberg's critical dead ends). I have come before you neither to denounce nor celebrate the ubiquity of popular music but to exploit and work with its everydayness—to see popular music as a privileged biopolitical operating system for examining cultural production and subject-formation in the twentieth and twenty-first centuries. The task I've set myself in this book is to take popular music seriously, not as a rarified set of highly meaningful aesthetic objects but as a common or everyday series of aesthetic practices, operations, or forms of life. I've set out here not to discover what popular music means but to examine how it functions, what kind of alternative "cognitive map" it might offer through the cultural life of recent decades. And as such, I hope to meet everyday popular music fans and critics where they already are, in the midst of a sea of listening.

Of course, it's the actual practice of listening to music that has changed most substantially in the past twenty or thirty years, in the shift from discipline to biopower. Certainly musical taste continues to do some subjective sorting work through a kind of excorporative method, but the thing that's changed quite radically in recent decades is the function of popular music in everyday life (rather than the discourse that surrounds it, which I agree with Grossberg hasn't changed substantially since its terms were set up by the Benjamin-Adorno debate in the 1930s). Over the past two decades, the disciplinary analog apparatus of listening to physical records or CDs (the immersive experience of listening to an entire album, consuming music on the analogy of reading a book) has been completely revolutionized by the MP3 playlist and the internet stream. And thereby music becomes less something to be consumed or interpreted, something that either positively or negatively offers meaning to our lives. Rather, music becomes more something that is used by dividuals and other collective actors to create various 'scapes in our individual and social lives—the sleep scape, the gym scape, the study scape, the commute scape, the romance scape, the political rally scape, the shopping scape. There are all kinds of playlists or internet streams for Saturday night as well as for Sunday morning.

Music theorist Anahid Kassabian calls this "ubiquitous listening," an ambient redistribution of music across the surface of our entire biopolitical lives, as opposed to thinking of the song as an individualized art form (on the analogy of the book or visual art work) to which listeners pay particularly dense aural attention—huddled in front of the record player with some friends, decoding the hidden messages of Pink Floyd's *Dark Side of the Moon* or intently trying to identify all the samples in De La Soul's *3 Feet High and Rising*. That's not how the vast majority of listening happens today. As music has saturated our entire lives, the kind of attention we pay to it inexorably changes as well, and this, as Kassabian argues, should give rise to "a whole new field of music studies, in which we stop thinking about compositional process, or genre, or industrial factors as the central matters,"[2] and turn critical attention instead to the ways that the new listening technology "modulates our attentional capacities, . . . tunes our affective relationships to categories of identity, [and] . . . conditions our participation in fields of subjectivity."[3] The ubiquitous, ambient music-scapes that Brian Eno dreamed of in the 1970s—in his *Music for Airports*, for example—have become the mundane reality of our MP3-packed lives only half a century later. And thereby the primary function of music has changed substantially—music is no longer primarily something that offers group or individual meaning or identity through excorporative distinction but more something that allows us to make our way through distributed fields of fluid subjectivity, surfing the modulations of late-late capitalist life, deploying just the right kind and levels of attention, focus, and distraction.

Of course, this question of distraction and its relations to capitalism brings us squarely back to Adorno, for whom distraction is precisely the function of popular music in late capitalist society. As Adorno writes in his classic, "On the Fetish-Character in Music and the Regression of Listening," "the categories of . . . art have no applicability to the contemporary reception of music" because art for Adorno requires something other than more of the same, something challenging and new.[4] Music's former artistic function, to unleash "the productive impulses which rebelled against conventions,"[5] has been obliterated "in capitalist times," wherein "the listener is converted, along his line of least resistance, into the acquiescent purchaser,"[6] and thereby pop music primarily provides shelter from the pity and awe that art is supposed to inspire. Here, popular music does not serve an artistic purpose but merely functions as "good entertainment and diversion":[7] not encouraging the listener's feelings of resistance to and autonomy from the dictates of the social whole but recruiting all listeners under the most basic tenet of capitalism— consume, don't do. In the end, for Adorno, "the liquidation of the individual is the real signature of the new musical situation":[8] despite "official culture's pretense of individualism," "the identical character of the goods which everyone must buy hides itself behind the rigor of the universally compulsory style,"[9] and the culture of supposed "individualism" and "taste" becomes merely hip commodity consumption. Popular music, Adorno concludes, "no longer produces any resistance" to the smooth functioning of mass culture's stultifying normative dictates.[10]

Fast-forward through Adorno's or Bourdieu's disciplinary society into a biopolitical control society, and it may be that distraction has some new, antihegemonic work to do. Indeed, the whole vocabulary of ambient, distracted consciousness has recently found itself inverted from its role as the Adornian bad guy, with distraction today constituting one of the utopian hopes for resistance in the present—functioning against the days of our hyperintense attention economy. "Ambience" as a critical concept has in the past decade found itself repurposed from Eno's work of the 1970s. Today, ambient music is no longer thought of primarily as a maneuver to reenchant drab disciplinary spaces like airports; rather, this new ambience functions as a kind of deterritorialized aesthetic consciousness that slowly traverses the surfaces of things like the "Sombre Reptiles" of Eno's *Another Green World*. I'm thinking here of a disparate set of aesthetic and theoretical deployments of ambience in recent cultural and theoretical production, everything from Chinese American poet Tan Lin's "ambient poetics" (which is a phrase also deployed in Timothy Morton's recent work on ecology) to Thomas Rickert's *Ambient Rhetoric*; or in literary criticism, consider the recent interest in ambient-style forms of reading that don't depend on close attention to seeking out and unearthing the hidden meaning behind textual details: surface reading, distant reading, descriptive reading, or postcritical reading. Or consider the Zen-like, nearly endless lists of stuff in so-called object-oriented ontology—birdcages and bowling balls and clown masks and cigarette butts.[11]

These are all attempts, it seems to me, to deal with and give form to an emergent "distracted" kind of aesthetic attention— one that refuses to focus on the last remaining neodisciplinary jobs of getting with the program or paying close attention to the task at hand. Because that's what advertisers and employers want from you: attention, and they want it 24/7. In a world where business gurus and TED-talkers alike remind us that "attention is the only worthwhile commodity of our time," the ubiquitous practice of an ear-budded musical distraction may serve a retooled utopian function in the present, if only as offering a momentary respite from the just-in-time, which is to say all-the-time, dictates of virtual attention capitalism.

"Well," the skeptical reader might reply, "putting together a 'killer workout playlist' isn't much of a form of resistance to multinational capital." Which is, I suppose, true enough, but it likewise seems to me that the whole category of resistance, like the sibling category of authenticity, may need to be updated in talking about and responding to present forms of capitalism. But if the ambient 'scaping of sounds, through playlists or streams, seems to you like capitulation rather than some sort of carving out a space within everyday neoliberal life, I'd at least ask you to consider the odd fact that a series of other cultural productions—poetry, rhetoric, literary criticism, philosophy, environmentalism—now find themselves aspiring to the ambient quality of music.

Or think of it this way, and this will be for me the final argumentative turn of the screw: when it comes to thinking about the legacy and history of cultural distraction, Adorno's beef with popular music was most definitively *not* that it merely delivered distraction from capitalist dictates. Rather, Adorno's critique is that music consistently *refused or failed to deliver* such distraction; as he writes in *Dialectic of Enlightenment*, it remains "doubtful whether the culture industry even still fulfills its self-proclaimed function of distraction."[12] Which is to say, popular music for Adorno failed to offer its listener any kind of aesthetic zone at least temporarily twisted free from the most obvious and craven dictates of capitalist life (in Adorno's time, the iron command to conform). Ironically, however, that's precisely one of the things that the MP3 or the internet stream offers to subjects today, regardless of its artistic "content" or whether anything in the playlist is intellectually challenging as music. That music would offer a subjectivity-twisting aesthetic challenge to the listener, Adorno's brass ring, is no longer quite to the point, simply because very few people are listening intently to the music anyway. People today primarily use music for things other than judging the excellence of music.

And this is also the brass ring problem for all forms of "post-critical reading": what are people going to read for if it's not for "meaning"? Why read at all, if it's just about a vague ambient feeling that music can more intensely and immediately invoke? Literary critics and contemporary authors can and do make claims for reading novels as a bulwark against the neoliberal fetishization of the present by referencing the fact that the immersive time of a sentence is hard to transactionalize; when we read, in short, we fall or drop out of the world of getting and spending into another temporality. As author Adam Haslett puts it in an interview on NPR, "The world is so insanely complex and fast and distracting, and one of the things I think a good book can do is slow the reader's attention down a little bit and give them a chance to think through some of the consequences of these changes which otherwise are so quick that all you can do is react."[13] True enough, but if that's the case (if reading's critique of capitalism lies in our escaping for a while the go-go present of consuming), then it seems to me that the stream or the playlist functions much more effectively than reading toward creating an ambient 'scaping of temporary autonomous spaces within contemporary life.

Maybe the problem with musical aesthetics since Benjamin and Adorno is not that music or music criticism is too bourgeois but that music and its criticism largely failed to deliver any of the supposed gains of musical aesthetics (a momentary musical respite from the dictates of capitalist life) to anyone other than the bourgeois class (who could learn through aesthetic judgment to take its distance from the commodified banality of everyday life). And that more democratic offering of a momentary buffer from the dictates of capitalism's attention economy may be what these various forms of ambient attention are trying to harness for the distracted consciousness of the twenty-first century. From philosophy and literary criticism, through poetry all the way to environmentalism: whatever these wide-ranging social and artistic formations are trying to leverage by thinking through distracted ambience as a way forward in contemporary late-late capitalist society, I'd at least like to insist that music was there first and offers the most obvious template for going forward in thinking about bulwarks against the dictates of biopolitical attention capitalism.

As Dominic Pettman writes in *Infinite Distraction*, a renewed sense of ambient musical (dis)engagement might "propose the possibility, or project, of fostering a *centripetal* form of distraction (i.e., as something more enmeshed than sheer dispersal, allowing a self-reflexive type of engagement which avoids the overdetermined mode of experience known as *attention*)."[14] In the end, I can only second Pettman's sense that "we should accept this challenge to rethink distraction as a potential ally" in the everyday fight against biopolitical capitalism and its all-the-time attention economy.[15] Indeed, this harnessing of distraction as a weapon against the colonizing forces of power has constituted an ongoing, but largely underdeployed, utopian possibility throughout the history of modern cultural studies. Think, for example, of Benjamin's musings concerning the potential political upshot of modern "reception in distraction": "The sort of distraction that is provided by art represents a covert measure of the extent to which it has become possible to perform new tasks of apperception."[16] In short, what looks like mere musical distraction may be the beginnings of a potentially oppositional form of cultural practice: one that helps us to understand attention and distraction as a mass cultural phenomenon, an ecology we inhabit rather than an individual disposition we choose.

As Yves Citton argues in *The Ecology of Attention*, a kind of distracted attention may be "holding out the promise of an EMANCIPATORY DISTRACTION: if we cannot be attentive enough [because of the sheer volume of cultural stuff that's out there], let us be attentive differently—and *make our distraction into an opportunity for a detachment which, freeing us from our voluntarist blinkers, will allow us to reconsider the problem in an entirely new way.*"[17] And that new way of thinking about attention and distraction may help us to think past the subjectivity traps of the twentieth century—the Adornian sense that it's only rare, authentic individuals who know how to rise above the fray of the shiny objects designed to draw the inauthentic attention of the masses. What we pay attention to in the internet age, as Jacques Lacan could have told us had he lived long enough, has everything to do with what the others are paying attention to. Thereby, we need to learn to pay attention to attention as a mass demographic or social phenomenon, not an individual choice. Insofar as we live in an environment of attention—we're soaking in it—Citton reminds us that "the detachment brought about by free-floating attention—whether it is rooted in a voluntary effort or in simple distraction through a lack of attentional resources—allows our joint (but unstuck) attention to discover forms, properties and potentialities that were not previously available to any of the individuals in the group."[18] Attention is a sea we live on and surf rather than a scarce resource we need to hoard, and musical detachment (as well as renewed forms of musical focus) may offer us ways of speeding up or slowing down those constant flows of distributed, ambient cultural attention.

Or if that utopian thesis seems a bit far-fetched, consider

Meaghan Morris's feminist plea, in her essay "Banality in Cultural Studies," to rethink distraction as something other than a confirmation of the Adornian thesis that those distracted by popular art forms are "cultural dopes." As Morris counters, "One could claim that this interpretation is possible only if one continues to assume that the academic traditions of 'contemplation' really do define intelligence, and that to be 'distracted' can therefore only mean being 'dopey'."[19] Likewise, unless we rethink this relation between contemplation (understood as good, autonomous, resistant, meaningful) and distraction (bad, enslaved, hoodwinked, meaningless) when it comes to contemporary artistic production, about all we can do going forward is to recycle the "way cool/sold out" dialectic that, as we have seen, has become a cul-de-sac for thinking about popular music practices. As Morris insists, "No matter which of the terms we validate, the contemplation/distraction, academic/popular oppositions can serve only to limit and distort the possibilities of popular practice."[20] And in the end, it is precisely through attending to the *practices* and *uses* of listening (rather than focusing on what popular music "means" within our lives) that we might be able to locate whatever hopes or fears accrue to the conflicted, everyday life of sound—possibilities or pitfalls for biopolitical subjects like us, who increasingly require practices that offer respite from our contemporary biopolitical enslavement to making and remaking our identities in every moment of our waking lives.

Or maybe what I'm arguing for here is, to borrow some lingo from Eve Kosofsky Sedgwick, a kind of "reparative" (rather than "paranoid") style of aesthetic engagement, one that looks to cultural productions for something other than depth, hidden meaning, or large-scale significance. As Sedgwick puts it, summing up Melanie Klein's work on the paranoid and the depressive, "the paranoid position . . . is a position of terrible alertness,"[21] always tasked with paying close attention so that one is not duped into playing the fool or making the same mistake over and over again. In listening parlance, authenticity-obsessed "rockist" listeners are resolutely paranoid, as they must always guard against being hoodwinked into investing in the wrong kind of "inauthentic" music, thereby putting precious cultural and social capital at stake. But Sedgwick (perhaps counterintuitively) finds a kind of queer potential not within that paranoid mindset but within a "depressive" aesthetic engagement (what we're translating as a set of ear-budded practices to fight off attention capitalism): "by contrast, the depressive position is an anxiety-mitigating achievement" that opens "the position from which it is possible in turn to use one's own resources to assemble or 'repair'" the paranoid space of constant subjective authenticity policing, or the contemporary overflow of way too many shiny objects vying for our attention.[22]

Though of course here I can see the paranoid retort coming back again strong for a lighter-raised-in-the-air encore, one . . . more . . . time: in short, the ultimate objection to such a position is that an ear-budded aesthetic space of involuted pleasure or mere escape is the *problem* rather than the *solution* in terms of the privatizing neoliberal imperatives dominant in contemporary capitalist life. The revolution can't come about if everyone's walled off in an isolated ambient environment. To that dismissal, Sedgwick offers a final (and to my mind definitive) rebuff, which is worth quoting at length:

> Reparative motives, once they become explicit, are inadmissible in paranoid theory both because they are about pleasure ("merely aesthetic") and because they are frankly ameliorative ("merely reformist"). What makes pleasure and amelioration so "mere"? Only the exclusiveness of paranoia's faith in demystifying exposure: only its cruel and contemptuous

assumption that the one thing lacking for global revolution, explosion of gender roles, or whatever, is people's (that is, other people's) having the painful effects of their oppression, poverty, or deludedness sufficiently exacerbated to make the pain conscious (as if otherwise it wouldn't have been) and intolerable (as if intolerable situations were famous for generating excellent solutions).[23]

Amen, Eve. If they are to function as politically compelling, everyday cultural practices of whatever kind have to function first as a biopolitical bridge from here to there rather than primarily being deployed as a cultural cover for the outsized demystifying claims of tenure-line intellectuals. In short, you have to follow how cultural practices function before you can talk about what they mean, and the functions of cover and momentary escape (so intensely bound up with the practice of listening to music) constitute the nonconscious and collective bases for those things called individual and group agency. And while it seems clear that "The Revolution Will Not Be Televised" for all the corporate-media reasons that Gil Scott-Heron laid out for us in his 1970 song, in the future the revolution may be available for a free download. Or at least its soundtrack will be.

In any case, as I've argued throughout *I'm Not Like Everybody Else*, thinking about popular music as the operating system of biopower, or as a kind of cognitive map for charting the territory of neoliberal biopolitics, is not so much a question of hope or despair but a matter of looking for new tools. So what tools does a biopolitical analysis offer us in terms of diagnosing the present? I would argue that the primary new tool on display here is one and the same with the new diagnosis—that the terrain of the disciplinary society has been permanently transformed and that we live in a vastly different world from the disciplinary world of training, enclosure, and confinement. We live instead in a world where we are enslaved to the very project of always modifying, updating, and retooling our lives—the very thing that the disciplinary society fought to keep at bay. Hence, all the ways that we thought of ourselves as being confined and/or freed have given way to a kind of ubiquitous governmentality under contemporary capitalism. We are literally a series of dividual relays among a series of machinic flows. And listening is a privileged practice where we meet, resist, and rework neoliberal social power, right on the surface of our everyday lives.

NOTES

INTRODUCTION

1. Lawrence Grossberg, "Reflections of a Disappointed Popular Music Scholar," in *Rock Over the Edge*, ed.   Roger Beebee, Denise Fulbrook, and Ben Saunders (Durham NC: Duke University Press, 2002), 28–29.

2. Andreas Huyssen, *After the Great Divide: Modernism, Mass Culture, Postmodernism* (Bloomington: Indiana University Press, 1987).

3. Theodor Adorno, "On Popular Music," in *Essays on Music*, ed. Richard Leppert, trans. Susan H. Gillespie (Berkeley: University of California Press, 2002), 442.

4. In the "33⅓" series of books on albums, see Gina Arnold's book on Liz Phair's *Exile in Guyville* (London: Bloomsbury, 2014) and Miles Marshall Lewis's book on Sly and the Family Stone's *There's a Riot Goin' On* (London: Bloomsbury, 2006).

5. Keir Keightley, "Reconsidering Rock," in *The Cambridge Companion to Pop and Rock*, ed. Simon Frith, Will Straw, and John Street (Cambridge: Cambridge University Press, 2001), 109.

6. Keightley, "Reconsidering Rock," 128.

1. BIOPOWER BLUES

1. Read about it here: www.nytimes.com/2013/06/16/world/asia/chinas -great-uprooting-moving-250-million-into-cities.html.

2. Václav Havel, "The Power of the Powerless," in *The Power of the Powerless: Citizens Against the State in Central-Eastern Europe*, quoted in Michael Weiss, "Vaclav Havel: Rock 'n' Roll and the Power of the Powerless," *World Affairs*, http://www.worldaffairsjournal.org

/article/vaclav-havel-rock-%e2%80%99n%e2%80%99-roll-and
-power-powerless.

3. Michel Foucault, *"Society Must Be Defended": Lectures at the College de France, 1975–76*, trans. David Macey (New York: Picador, 2003), 242.

4. Michel Foucault, *Discipline and Punish*, trans. Alan Sheridan (New York: Vintage, 1979), 138.

5. Michel Foucault, *The Birth of Biopolitics: Lectures at the College de France 1978–79*, trans. Graham Burchell (New York: Picador, 2010), 259–60.

6. David Hesmondhalgh, *Why Music Matters* (London: Wiley-Blackwell, 2013), 1–2.

7. Hesmondhalgh, *Why Music Matters*, 2.

8. Hesmondhalgh, *Why Music Matters*, 2.

9. Simon Frith, "Music and Identity," in *Questions of Cultural Identity*, ed. Stuart Hall and Paul du Gay (London: Sage, 1996), 110.

2. STEAL YOUR FACE

1. You can see it here (the Dead come up at around the thirty-two -minute mark): https://www.youtube.com/watch?v=d-UOMp RYPAM.

2. As Keightley points out in "Reconsidering Rock," claims to the special status of youth were key to the ideology of 1960s musical authenticity and opposition: "If 'youth' was opposed to 'adult,' and the 'adult' was responsible for 'mass society,' then 'youth' could understand itself as inherently 'anti-mass,' regardless of how many million rock records were sold" (124); likewise, the supposed authentic, antimass nature of youth allowed suburban white kids to express a completely unearned solidarity with other minorities frowned upon by the repressive "adult" mainstream.

3. See Gilles Deleuze's essay "Postscript on Societies of Control," *October* 59 (Winter 1992), 5.

4. "Margaret Thatcher: A Life in Quotes," *Guardian*, April 8, 2013, https://www.theguardian.com/politics/2013/apr/08/margaret -thatcher-quotes.

5. From Reagan's first inaugural address, January 20, 1981: http://www .presidency.ucsb.edu/ws/?pid=43130.

6. David Dodd, "The Annotated 'Ripple,'" in *The Annotated Grateful Dead Lyrics*, http://artsites.ucsc.edu/gdead/agdl/ripple.html.

7. See Lazzarato's *Signs and Machines: Capitalism and the Production of Subjectivity*, trans. J. D. Jordan (Cambridge MA: MIT Press, 2014).

8. γένοι' οἷος ἐσσὶ μαθών—https://en.wikiquote.org/wiki/Pindar.

9. Felix Guattari, *Molecular Revolution*, trans. Rosemary Sheed (New York: Penguin, 1984), 171.

10. Gilles Deleuze, *Difference and Repetition*, trans. Paul Patton (New York: Columbia University Press, 1995), 100.

11. Pierre Bourdieu, *Distinction: A Social Critique of the Judgment of Taste*, trans. Richard Nice (Cambridge MA: Harvard University Press, 1984), 18.

3. NOT FOR SALE

1. Joseph Heath and Andrew Potter, *Nation of Rebels: Why Counterculture Became Consumer Culture* (New York: Harper Business, 2004), 3.

4. A GENEALOGY OF POPULAR MUSIC

1. Shannon Winnubst, *Way Too Cool: Selling Out Race and Ethics* (New York: Columbia University Press, 2015), 3.

2. Tricia Rose, *The Hip Hop Wars* (Boston: Basic Books, 2008), 223.

3. Amiri Baraka (LeRoi Jones), *Blues People: The Negro Experience in White America and the Music that Developed from It* (New York: William Morrow, 1963), 191.

4. Baraka, *Blues People*, 192.

5. Baraka, *Blues People*, 188.

6. Baraka, *Blues People*, 154.

5. GOOD ROCKIN' TONITE

1. Greil Marcus, *Mystery Train: Images of America in Rock 'n' Roll Music* (New York: Plume, 2008), 144.

2. Marcus, *Mystery Train*, 145.

3. Marcus, *Mystery Train*, 145.

4. See especially Richard Peterson, "Why 1955? Explaining the Advent of Rock Music," *Popular Music* 9, no. 1 (1990): 97–116.

5. Watch it here: https://www.youtube.com/watch?v=iWj7bLxM0zg .

6. Watch it here: https://www.youtube.com/watch?v=omn-1nsqv3u.

7. Watch the performance, as well as Sullivan's contextualization of it, here: https://www.youtube.com/watch?v=s_quozub0wY.

8. Cited in Elijah Wald, *How the Beatles Destroyed Rock 'n' Roll* (New York: Oxford University Press, 2011), 199.

9. Keir Keightley, "Reconsidering Rock," in *The Cambridge Companion to Pop and Rock*, ed. Simon Frith, Will Straw, and John Street (Cambridge: Cambridge University Press, 2001), 115.

10. See Wald, *How the Beatles*, 204.

11. Simon Frith, "'The Magic That Can Set You Free': The Ideology of Folk and the Myth of the Rock Community," *Popular Music* 1, no. 1 (1981), 159–60.

12. Frith, "'The Magic That Can Set You Free,'"160.

13. Frith, "'The Magic That Can Set You Free,'"162.

14. Frith, "'The Magic That Can Set You Free,'" 164.

15. On the rise (and fall) of the rock star as a template or driver for mass subjectivity, see David Shumway, *Rock Star: The Making of Musical Icons from Elvis to Springsteen* (Baltimore: Johns Hopkins University Press, 2014).

6. MUSICAL COMMUNITY

1. Lawrence Grossberg, "Reflections of a Disappointed Popular Music Scholar," in *Rock Over the Edge*, ed. Roger Beebee, Denise Fulbrook, and Ben Saunders (Durham NC: Duke University Press, 2002), 44.

2. Pierre Bourdieu, *Distinction: A Social Critique of the Judgment of Taste*, trans. Richard Nice (Cambridge MA: Harvard University Press, 1984), 56.

3. Garcia lays out his excorporative reasoning in this short snippet from an interview: https://www.youtube.com/watch?v=Q1RaBdSCjAY.

4. Keir Keightley, "Reconsidering Rock," in *The Cambridge Companion to Pop and Rock*, ed. Simon Frith, Will Straw, and John Street (Cambridge: Cambridge University Press, 2001), 125.

5. Greil Marcus, *Lipstick Traces: A Secret History of the Twentieth Century* (Cambridge MA: Harvard University Press, 1990), 57.

6. Watch the whole show here: https://www.youtube.com/watch?v=qbvdsz5qd6g.

7. Read the poem here: http://www.nathanielturner.com/blackart.htm.

8. On the rebranding of punk as alternative, see Thomas Frank, "Alternative to What?" originally published in *The Baffler 5* (December 1993): https://thebaffler.com/salvos/alternative-to-what.

9. Dick Hebdige, *Subculture: The Meaning of Style* (London: Routledge, 1979), 105.

10. Hebdige, *Subculture*, 111.

11. Hebdige, *Subculture*, 125.

12. Hebdige, *Subculture*, 119.

13. Hebdige, *Subculture*, 126.

14. Marcus, *Lipstick Traces*, 9.

15. Walter Benjamin, "The Work of Art in the Age of Its Technological Reproducibility (Third Version)," trans. Harry Zohn and Edmund Jephcott, in *Selected Writings, Volume 4 (1938–1940)*, eds. Howard Eiland and Michael W. Jennings, trans. Edmund Jephcott and Others (Cambridge MA: Harvard University Press), 269.

16. Gilles Deleuze and Felix Guattari, *A Thousand Plateaus: Capitalism and Schizophrenia, Volume 2*, trans. Brian Massumi (Minneapolis: University of Minnesota Press, 1980), 299, 348.

17. Bourdieu, *Distinction*, 80.

18. Barry Shank, *The Political Force of Musical Beauty* (Durham NC: Duke University Press, 2014), 3.

19. Shank, *Political Force of Musical Beauty*, 16.

20. Shank, *Political Force of Musical Beauty*, 260.

21. Shank, *Political Force of Musical Beauty*, 150–51.

22. Keightley, "Reconsidering Rock," 137.

23. Watch it here: https://www.youtube.com/watch?v=h_ivjAqYB68 —the moment I discuss in chapter 6 comes at the 1.29 mark, as Davies invites the audience to join him in singing biopower's refrain. The most Nuremberg-ish shot comes in the applause after the song is over.

24. Keightley, "Reconsidering Rock," 133.

25. Jacques Attali, *Noise: The Political Economy of Music*, trans. Brian Massumi (Minneapolis: University of Minnesota Press, 1984), 5.

26. Attali, *Noise*, 5.

27. Attali, *Noise*, 144.

28. Attali, *Noise*, 9.

29. Attali, *Noise*, 11.

7. CAPITALISM, FROM MEANING TO USAGE

1. Michel Foucault, "Space, Power, Knowledge," in *The Cultural Studies Reader*, ed. Simon During (London and New York: Routledge, 2007), 136.

2. Read the sad story here: http://www.rollingstone.com/music/news /kiss-paul-stanley-says-ace-frehley-threw-away-incredible-potential -20140303.

3. Simon Frith, "'The Magic That Can Set You Free': The Ideology of Folk and the Myth of the Rock Community," *Popular Music* 1, no. 1 (1981), 161.

4. The essay in question is Nietzsche's "On Truth and Lie in a Non-Moral Sense," http://nietzsche.holtof.com/Nietzsche_various/on _truth_and_lies.htm.

5. Simon Frith, "Pet Shop Boys: The Divine Commodity," *Village Voice Rock and Roll Quarterly* (Spring 1988): 147-48, https://rockcritics .com/2014/01/13/pet-shop-boys-critically-7/.

6. Robin James, *Resilience and Melancholy: Pop Music, Feminism, Neoliberalism* (Winchester, UK: Zero Books, 2015).

7. Tom Vanderbilt, *You May Also Like: Taste in an Age of Endless Choice* (New York: Knopf, 2016), 97.

8. Pierre Bourdieu, *Distinction: A Social Critique of the Judgment of Taste*, trans. Richard Nice (Cambridge MA: Harvard University Press, 1984), 375.

9. Dan Fox, *Pretentiousness: Why It Matters* (New York: Coffee House Press, 2016), 104.

10. Vanderbilt, *You May Also Like*, 98.

11. Vanderbilt, *You May Also Like*, 98.

12. Vanderbilt, *You May Also Like*, 108.

13. Quoted in Vanderbilt, *You May Also Like*, 111.

8. IN THE MOOD

1. Theodor Adorno and Max Horkheimer, *Dialectic of Enlightenment*, trans. Edmund Jephcott (Stanford: Stanford University Press, 2007), 97.

2. Paul Allen Anderson, "Neo-Muzak and the Business of Mood," *Critical Inquiry* 41, no. 4 (2015), 811.

3. Anderson, "Neo-Muzak," 839.

4. Anderson, "Neo-Muzak," 837.

5. Carolyn Dicey Jennings, "I Attend, Therefore I Am: You Are Only as Strong as Your Powers of Attention," *Aeon: A World of Ideas*, July 10, 2017, https://aeon.co/essays/what-is-the-self-if-not-that-which-pays-attention.

6. Jonathan Beller, "Paying Attention," *Cabinet* 24 (2006–7), http://www.cabinetmagazine.org/issues/24/beller.php.

7. Jonathan Beller, *The Cinematic Mode of Production: Attention Economy and the Society of the Spectacle* (Hanover NH: Dartmouth University Press, 2006), 4.

8. Beller, *Cinematic Mode of Production*, 27.

9. Beller, *Cinematic Mode of Production*, 3.

10. Jacques Attali, *Noise: The Political Economy of Music*, trans. Brian Massumi (Minneapolis: University of Minnesota Press, 1984), 3.

11. Listen to it here: https://www.youtube.com/watch?v=6NFDgl8TnUE.

12. On the function of the earworm, see Peter Szendy, *Hits: Philosophy in the Jukebox*, trans. Will Bishop (New York: Fordham University Press, 2012).

13. Tom Vanderbilt, *You May Also Like: Taste in an Age of Endless Choice* (New York: Knopf, 2016), 92.

9. WILL THERE BE MUSIC?

1. Specifically, Adorno writes in his 1949 essay "Cultural Criticism and Society": "Cultural criticism finds itself faced with the final stage of the dialectic of culture and barbarism. To write poetry after Auschwitz is barbaric. And this corrodes even the knowledge of why it has become impossible to write poetry today. Absolute reification, which presupposed intellectual progress as one of its elements, is now preparing to absorb the mind entirely." In his essay collection *Prisms*, trans. Samuel Weber and Shierry Weber Nicholsen (Cambridge MA: MIT Press, 1983), 34.

2. Jonathan Beller, *The Cinematic Mode of Production: Attention Economy and the Society of the Spectacle* (Hanover NH: Dartmouth University Press, 2006), 108.

3. Beller, *Cinematic Mode of Production*, 109.

4. Pierre Bourdieu, *Distinction: A Social Critique of the Judgment of Taste*, trans. Richard Nice (Cambridge MA: Harvard University Press, 1984), 30–31.

5. Bourdieu, *Distinction*, 31.

10. BOURDIEU, BOURDON'T

1. Pierre Bourdieu, *Distinction: A Social Critique of the Judgment of Taste*, trans. Richard Nice (Cambridge MA: Harvard University Press, 1984), 56.

2. Bourdieu, *Distinction*, 85–86.

3. Bourdieu, *Distinction*, 86.

4. Bourdieu, *Distinction*, 120.

5. Emily Jane Fox, "Let Fran Lebowitz Soothe All Your Election-Related Worries," *Vanity Fair*, October 20, 2016, http://www.vanityfair.com/news/2016/10/fran-lebowitz-trump-clinton-election.

6. Bourdieu, *Distinction*, 125.

7. Fox, "Fran Lebowitz."

8. Pierre Bourdieu, "Passport to Duke," in *Pierre Bourdieu: Fieldwork in Culture*, ed. Imre Szeman and Nicholas Brown (Lanham MD: Rowman & Littlefield, 2000), 245.

9. Bourdieu, *Distinction*, 16.

10. Bourdieu, *Distinction*, 63.

11. See on this topic Judith Butler, "Merely Cultural," *New Left Review* 227 (January–February 1998): 33–44.

12. See Shannon Winnubst's *Way Too Cool: Selling Out Race and Ethics* (New York: Columbia University Press, 2015) for a critique of Butler's work and the logic of neoliberalism: "Butler's theorizing of gender captures . . . a fundamental transformation underway in the neoliberal episteme: we are purely and only how we appear and the more interesting we can appear, the more successful and cooler we are! And gender, especially understood as the endless donning of cool new fashion accessories, is the most fabulous way to intensify our ever so cool appearances" (123). In short, "I argue that *Gender Trouble* may be a quintessentially neoliberal text" (125). That Butler's work was received in this way is of course true—neoliberalism as a cultural dominant is like that, laying out the conditions of reception for everything from pop music to high

theory; whether a hidden commitment to neoliberal capitalism inspires Butler's work is another question altogether.

13. Michel Foucault, *Foucault Live: Collected Interviews, 1961–1984*, ed. Sylvère Lotringer, trans. Lysa Hochroth and John Johnston (New York: Semiotext(e), 1996), 73.

11. EVERYWHERE, ALL THE TIME

1. Check out the numbers from the Pew Research Center here: http://www.pewinternet.org/fact-sheet/mobile/.

2. Anahid Kassabian, *Ubiquitous Listening: Affect, Attention, and Distributed Subjectivity* (Berkeley: University of California Press, 2013), 19.

3. Kassabian, *Ubiquitous Listening*, 18.

4. Theodor Adorno, "On the Fetish-Character in Music and the Regression of Listening," trans. Richard Leppert, in *Essays on Music*, ed. Richard Leppert (Berkeley: University of California Press, 2002), 289.

5. Adorno, "On the Fetish-Character," 290–91.

6. Adorno, "On the Fetish-Character," 291.

7. Adorno, "On the Fetish-Character," 292.

8. Adorno, "On the Fetish-Character," 293.

9. Adorno, "On the Fetish-Character," 297.

10. Adorno, "On the Fetish-Character," 310.

11. For a sense of Tan Lin's "ambient poetics," watch his "Eleven Minute Painting" and the discussion that follows here: https://www.youtube.com/watch?v=iHA_eX_hWek&t=1230s. For a discussion of ambient poetics within environmental discourse, see Timothy Morton's *Ecology without Nature* (Cambridge MA: Harvard University Press, 2007), 34–39. For a sense of various ambient-style forms of reading that don't depend on focused critical attention to hidden or obscured "meaning" within a particular text, see Franco Moretti, *Distant Reading* (London: Verso, 2013); Rita Felske, *The Limits of Critique* (Chicago: University of Chicago Press, 2015); Stephen Best and Sharon Marcus, "Surface Reading: An Introduction" in *Representations 108*, no.1 (Fall 2009): 1–21; and Heather Love, "Close but not Deep: Literary Ethics and the Descriptive Turn" in *New Literary History 41*, no. 2 (Spring 2010): 371–91. See also Thomas

Rickert, *Ambient Rhetoric* (Pittsburgh: University of Pittsburgh Press, 2013). The best Object-Oriented Ontology "book of ambient lists" is probably Ian Bogost, *Alien Phenomenology, or What It's Like to Be a Thing* (Minneapolis: University of Minnesota Press, 2012).

12. Theodor Adorno and Max Horkheimer, *Dialectic of Enlightenment*, trans. Edmund Jephcott (Stanford: Stanford University Press, 2007), 110.

13. Quoted in Jeffrey T. Nealon, *Post-Postmodernism: or, The Cultural Logic of Just-in-Time Capitalism* (Stanford CA: Stanford University Press, 2012), 151.

14. Dominic Pettman, *Infinite Distraction* (London: Polity Press, 2015), 134.

15. Pettman, *Infinite Distraction*, 136.

16. Walter Benjamin, "The Work of Art in the Age of Its Technological Reproducibility (Third Version)," trans. Harry Zohn and Edmund Jephcott, in *Selected Writings, Volume 4 (1938–1940)*, eds. Howard Eiland and Michael W. Jennings, trans. Edmund Jephcott and others (Cambridge MA: Harvard University Press), 268.

17. Yves Citton, *The Ecology of Attention*, trans. Barnaby Norman (Cambridge UK: Polity Press, 2017), 117 (emphasis and capitals in original).

18. Citton, *Ecology of Attention*, 119.

19. Meaghan Morris, "Banality in Cultural Studies," in *The Cultural Studies Reader*, 3rd ed., ed. Simon During (New York: Routledge, 2007), 129.

20. Morris, "Banality in Cultural Studies," 129.

21. Eve Kosofsky Sedgwick, "Paranoid Reading and Reparative Reading, or, You're So Paranoid, You Probably Think This Essay Is About You," in *Touching Feeling: Affect, Pedagogy, Performativity* (Durham NC: Duke University Press, 2003), 128.

22. Sedgwick, "Paranoid Reading," 128.

23. Sedgwick, "Paranoid Reading," 144.

To order or obtain more information on these or other University of
Nebraska Press titles, visit nebraskapress.unl.edu.

www.ingramcontent.com/pod-product-compliance
Ingram Content Group UK Ltd.
Pitfield, Milton Keynes, MK11 3LW, UK
UKHW042149060225
454777UK00004B/389